TRAILING WHITETAILS

TRAILING WHITETAILS

John Trout, Jr.

North Country Press · Unity, Maine

Library of Congress Cataloging-in-Publication Data:

Trout, John, 1946–
    Trailing whitetails.

    1. White-tailed deer hunting.   2. Bear hunting.
3. Black bear.   4. Tracking and trailing.   I. Title.
SK301.T75   1987   799.2'77357   87-22137
ISBN 0-945980-14-0 (formerly ISBN 0-89621-109-6) (alk. paper)

Cover photograph by Dennis Moseley.
Illustrations on pages 20 and 21 by Robert Pratt and
Wayne Trim from *Whitetail Deer Ecology and Management.*
Copyright © 1984 by Stackpole Books and Wildlife
Management Institute.

All other illustrations Copyright © 1987 by Larry Smail.

Book layout by Charles Fortier.
Composition by Camden Type 'n Graphics, Camden, Maine.
Cover design by Ralph Lizotte.
Second printing, 1989

To good ol' Dad.
Without him, I might never have known the outdoors
as I know it today.

ACKNOWLEDGMENTS

I have been fortunate to have spent the better part of my life hunting and admiring the whitetail deer. These special moments have become memories that will never be erased. These great times would not have been possible by just being there. It has taken the companionship of many others. I express special thanks to dad for introducing me to the great outdoors, and thanks to mom for her support on writing this book. Thanks to friends I have hunted with throughout the years, for without them the enjoyment might not have been the same. They are some of the best deer hunters going.

I would like to thank Lori Pruitt, Deer Research Biologist, Indiana Department Of Natural Resources, for contributing information that was very helpful to my book.

Many thanks to Dr. Philip S. Palutsis, physician and surgeon, of Westchester, Illinois, who spent a great deal of time answering valuable questions about the wounding affects on the whitetail deer.

For permission to reprint illustrations and material, I express thanks to the Wildlife Society, and to the Wildlife Management Institute. Also, thanks to The Game Tracker, Inc., for supplying me with information and accessories.

I thank Professor Aaron N. Moen for comments about wounding affects on the whitetail deer; Leonard Lee Rue Enterprises, for supplying many helpful photographs; and all my friends who contributed photographs.

Thanks to Larry Smail for doing a fine job with the splendid illustrations used throughout, a great asset to the book.

Special thanks to Janice Kopatich, Janet Metzger, and Colleen Talley, who did proof reading and helped correct the manuscript.

I thank my four children, Alisa, Tammy, Kathy, and John, for patience with my hunting throughout the years. This book would not have been possible without long hours spent in the field, perhaps times I should have been home instead. I apologize for any negligence they endured since I began the book, so many hours at my desk with the door closed.

Last, I want to thank my wife, Vikki, for all those suppers she kept warm while I was on a tracking job, for her patience and understanding over the years, for her help with the typewriter, and for serving as part-time editor.

CONTENTS

INTRODUCTION

I was first introduced to the hunting world when only eight years old, as I accompanied dad on a squirrel hunt. I have since loved any time spent in the outdoors. I went on to deer, turkey, and black bear hunting, and just about anything else that would put me in the field.

Over the years I found enjoyment in many ways. I realized it does not take a kill to make a hunt memorable. It is just being there. I have spent more countless hours just admiring the whitetail deer, finding it just as exciting to position myself on a soybean field with a camera, as with a weapon. But I do look forward to the kill, for it is like icing on the cake.

My first love has been bow hunting, the gun a close second, as bow hunting puts me a little closer to the animal. I have bow hunted and gun hunted the whitetail for the better part of 25 years, have enough experiences to last a lifetime, but still look forward to the next. I was fortunate to have been raised in some of Indiana's finest whitetail deer country. I remember when it was luck to see a deer during a week of hard hunting, simply

11

because deer were not around in great numbers. Today a hunter can not only count on seeing a lot of deer, but can be selective about what he shoots.

Over the years I have been involved in more than 300 experiences trailing wounded whitetails. Some resulted from deer I had shot, and many others were with hunting companions. This has given me a good insight, as well as a lot of fond memories. Several friends can trail a wounded deer as effectively or better than I can, nice friends to count on.

I had considered writing this book on trailing for several years, not because I had an ambition to get rich from it, but because I wanted to share the knowledge and experiences. As I began writing, I soon realized a need for outside help. I put a great deal of research into the subject by contacting many other qualified persons, and learned much more.

You will see that I did not leave out the suffering. I simply tell it like it really is. Any discussion that deals with a wounded animal is a touchy one, particularly for the anti-hunter to accept. However, I think that a lot of good will come out of this book and help a beginning or experienced hunter to become more responsible. It will teach the practice of proper shot placement, as well as advanced trailing techniques. It will help reduce the number of whitetails that may rot away, because of an irresponsible hunter.

This book does not focus on just bow hunting, or just gun hunting, as probable reactions to each are discussed. Both are humane weapons in the hands of the right people. The person who carries the weapon determines how much suffering will be involved. Whether we hunt for meat or sport, the intent should be to kill as quickly and humanely as possible; shoot only when confident of a kill, and do everything humanly possible to recover the animal. If a whitetail has been poorly hit, it is up to the shooter to put time into the recovery. No animal should be given up unless the hunter is absolutely sure it was only a superficial wound, and the animal will most likely recover. Although we have heard this over and over, some still fail to practice it. Deer that die and are left unrecovered do not deserve to perish for no reason. This is simply more ammunition for the anti-hunter. If you feel that the deer you have shot will die, don't give up until you have put forth every possible effort in an attempt to recover it. It is not always the blood trail that leads to a deer, many times it's just plain old determination.

A lot of opinions have been given on the theory of "how long to wait before taking up the trail of a wounded whitetail." This is a very important decision the hunter must make, one that could determine the outcome of the situation. Many articles have been published concerning this, and many opinions given. I shall express my opinion, and I am confident I am correct. It is not the reading of articles that has taught me, but years of deer hunting experience.

I believe you will gain the most from this book by reading it from start to finish, rather than jumping around to areas of particular interest. It would take many years in the field to learn what you can in just a short reading time. I welcome any response from readers, and enjoy hearing about unique and different trailing experiences. We all still have a lot to learn.

CHAPTER 1

ANATOMY AND SHOT PLACEMENT

*T*he most graceful movements of the whitetail deer (*Obocoileus virginianus*) has amazed many of us from time to time. We deer hunters, while in pursuit of this magnificent animal, have spent countless hours admiring the whitetail.

They are an excellent design of bone, muscle, and tissue with the end result a perfectly co-ordinated body which enables them to undertake things we humans could never begin to endure. However, we have one advantage that the whitetail does not have, the ability to think and reason. We are the dominant species, so we are the hunters and the whitetail is the hunted.

The whitetail has two things in life to cope with: survival and reproduction. Its instinct is to survive, which keeps it alive, but on occasion an instinct to reproduce may bring death. But even though the deer hunter is being given more opportunity than ever before to learn and study his quarry, the whitetail continues to flourish in abundance.

15

Anyone who puts an effort into deer hunting wants to be successful, logically speaking. Some put a tremendous amount of hours into pre-season scouting and read everything available on the subject of deer hunting. We are given many opportunities to study biological research done on the whitetail, but it still boils down to one instant which decides success or failure. That moment of truth is "the shot".

Before the shot is taken, we have to know when and at what to shoot. Some beginning hunters are merely satisfied to shoot at the body, usually around the middle section, yet this seems to offer the most room for error, and leads to crippling. The bow hunter must pick a spot, just as the gun hunter who looks down the cross hairs of a scope. This is when to know for sure what spot should be picked, and exactly where the spot is located.

When a deer hunter pulls the trigger or releases an arrow, it has to be with the intent to kill as quickly and humanely as possible. In order to do this, it is important to know the vital organs that offer the quickest kill.

It is important to study all of the internal organs, vital and non-vital, and know what offers the largest and the quickest killing target, also what organs are considered vital and what are non-vital.

The organs that offer the quickest killing shots are the lungs, heart, and kidneys. The egg-shaped kidneys would certainly be a poor target, since the adult whitetail kidney measures only about $3^1/2$ by $2^1/2$ inches.

This leaves the lungs and heart as the prime target. The nice thing is that they are both located close together inside the chest diaphragm. The adult whitetail's inflated lungs, are about nine inches in length and six inches in width, to offer a target approximately the size of a football.

Any shot through the front shoulders or up to five inches behind the shoulder will almost certainly strike the lungs, providing the shot is not too far forward or too high.

The adult whitetail heart measures about six inches in length by about four inches in width and resembles the shape of a grapefruit. Many hunters think the heart is the deadliest organ

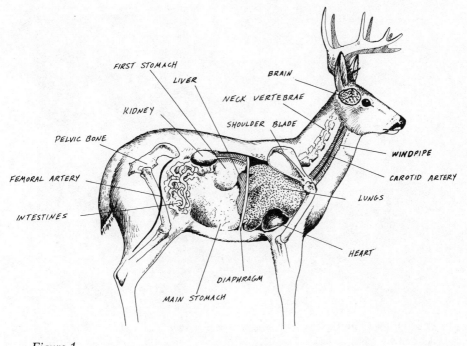

Figure 1
All of the internal organs, vital and non-vital.
Illustration by Larry Smail.

and that they should aim for it, but in all reality this just isn't so. True, it will certainly cause a quick death, but the lungs are just as deadly when punctured and will most definitely cause death just as quickly. Another way of looking at it is the fact that the heart lies low in the chest cavity and just above the elbow point of the front legs. Since it is a smaller target and would have to allow a lower aiming point, it becomes a greater risk of missing your target. The lungs, on the other hand, enable a hunter to aim on center of the deer's body width and, of course, stay forward towards the shoulder. This allows more room for error and still obtains a vital hit.

The liver, just behind the chest diaphragm, is also close to the vital lungs. Unfortunately, even though a liver hit will kill,

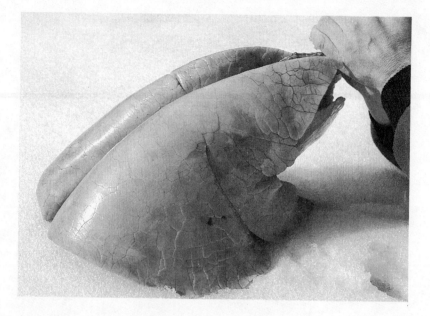

The inflated lungs of a 140 pound live weight whitetail.
Photo by Leonard Lee Rue III.

it is not as vital as the lungs. The hit liver takes much more time before the animal succumbs to death, and creates much more of a recovery problem. This will be discussed later.

The paunch section, which takes in the stomach and intestines, may also kill, but once again this creates the same hazards as does the liver hit, as far as trailing and recovery are concerned.

The major arteries will generally bleed out a deer in a matter of seconds. Since they only have a diameter of about one-half of an inch, they offer the hunter no shot whatsoever. When an artery is severed, it is usually by luck alone, and I admit there have been a few occasions when an artery hit helped to fill my tag.

We must look at shot placement from two aspects. The bow hunter, finds shot placement a more limited area than the gun hunter.

The razor sharp broadhead can kill as quickly as a bullet in most situations. I am a two-season advocate, hunting with bow and gun each year. I have managed many times to see the different methods of destruction that the broadhead and bullet can do.

The broadhead, providing it is razor sharp, will slice and cut through anything as long as enough power is backing it. The broadhead causes severe hemorrhaging while the bullet literally crushes, destructs, and mutilates everything in its path. The shocking power of a bullet is enough in itself to do great damage to a whitetail.

There have been times when I had my bow in hand, only to wish it were my favorite deer gun, when a buck offered no shot

The heart of a 170 pound field dressed whitetail buck.

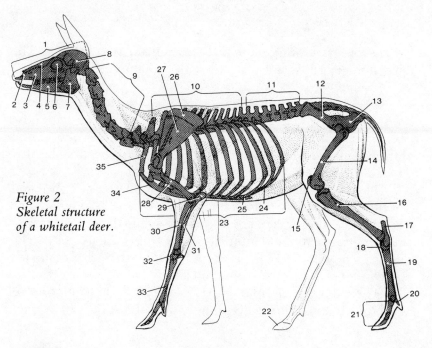

Figure 2
Skeletal structure
of a whitetail deer.

1 Skull	19 Metatarsus
2 Os incisivum	20 Dew Claw of Phalanges
3 Maxilla	21 Phalanges
4 Os nasale	22 Hoof
5 Mandible	23 Rib Cage
6 Orbita	24 Rib Cartilages
7 Mandibular condyle	25 Xiphoid cartilage
8 Os temporale	26 Scapula Cartilage
9 Cervical vertebrae	27 Scapula
10 Thoracic vertebrae	28 Humerus
11 Lumbar vertebrae	29 Olecranon
12 Ilium	30 Radius
13 Ischium	31 Ulna
14 Femur	32 Carpals
15 Patella	33 Metacarpal
16 Tibia	34 Sternum
17 Tuber calcis	35 First Rib
18 Tarsus	

Illustrations by Robert Pratt and Wayne Trimm.

20

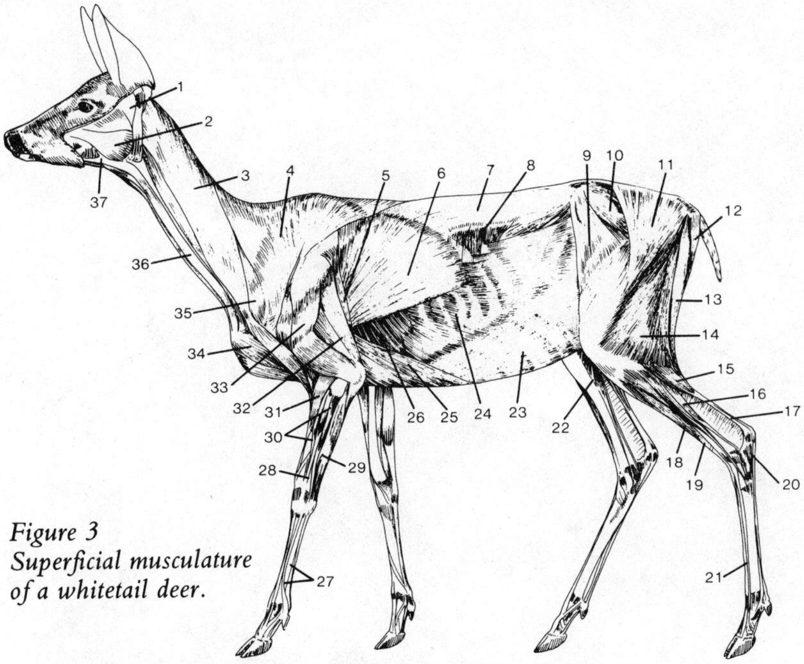

Figure 3
Superficial musculature
of a whitetail deer.

1 Arcus zygomaticus
2 Masseter
3 Brachiocephalicus
4 Trapezius
5 Tensor fasciae antebrachii
6 Latissimus dorsi
7 Lumbo-dorsal fascis
8 Serratus ventralis
9 Tensor fasciae externus
10 Gluteus medius
11 Trochanter major
12 Semimembranosus
13 Semitendinosus
14 Biceps femoris
15 Gastrocnemius
16 Deep flexor tendon
17 Tendon of Achilles
18 Lasteral extensor
19 Long extensor

20 Superficial flexor tendon
21 Anterior tendon
22 Flexor digitorum (pedislongus)
23 Aponeurosis
24 Obliquus abdominis externus
25 Deep pectoral
26 Serratis ventralis
27 Flexor tendons of metatarsus
28 Tendon of extensor digiti
29 Extensor carpi (ulnaris)
30 Extensor digiti
31 Extensor carpi (radialis)
32 Triceps
33 Deltoid
34 Superficial pectoral (brisket)
35 Shoulder-transverse process muscle
36 Sternocephalicus
37 Sternomandibularis

Figure 4
Definitely not a shot for the bow hunter, but some cases for the gun hunter.
By Larry Smail.

at all for a bow hunter. There have also been times when I hit a whitetail with a gunshot that I would have gladly traded for a bow shot. Regardless, you have to know how to make the best of the situation, when the time comes. I firmly believe the most critical time on a hunt is just knowing when or when not to shoot. Realizing when to shoot means knowing your capabilities.

The gun hunter has to know his gun and know it well, its limitations as far as distance and trajectory are concerned.

The bow hunter must also know his equipment and his limitations. Some bow hunters may take shots at distances of 40 yards or more just because they are offered, even though their effective and accurate shooting range may be only 20 yards. I am a 15 to 20 yard shooter, and that is my limit. I have taken longer shots and lucked out on occasion, but it won't happen often. As long as I am aware of this, I can prevent a mistake before it happens.

The bow hunter must learn to control temptation on shots considered risky to his or her own ability. I firmly believe most animals are poorly hit by shots beyond a normal capability, either with gun or bow.

Another problem the bow hunter faces is shooting at unknown distances. Whitetails do not walk around with a white aiming patch on the side, announcing yardage from hunter to deer. I have seen bow hunters who group arrows all day long at 60 yards, but miss a whitetail standing broadside at 15 yards.

First we will look at the quartering-into shot. This is a poor ground shot and an extremely poor tree stand shot, one I feel the bow hunter should never attempt. The only aiming point is the shoulder, a tough entry for any arrow, even with heavy poundage. The angle is totally wrong and causes the arrow to veer away from the vitals instead of towards them.

Figure 5
This buck offers no shot for the bow hunter and in some cases is risky business for the gun hunter. By Larry Smail.

As a gun hunter, I would take this shot only if the deer was close and I was sure it would not turn broadside. If the animal is approaching my stand position, I would certainly wait for a better opportunity, providing it has not become aware of my presence.

The frontal shot would also be risky business unless the deer is extremely close to the gun hunter. This bow shot should not be attempted on the ground or from an elevated stand position unless the deer is extremely close and you are confident in shooting ability at that distance.

Figure 6
Aiming points are shown for the rear point of the spine and the femoral artery.
By Larry Smail.

Some hunters are tempted to take this shot when an oncoming deer suddenly realizes danger may be ahead and decides to put on the brakes. After a little foot stomping and staring in the direction ahead, it finally throws the head from side to side trying to figure out what's going on. Temptation builds up as the hunter realizes he will probably get no other shot. The truth is, we should forget about shooting this time. There is always a chance the deer may turn and offer a more promising shot.

Figure 7
The near-perfect shot for bow hunter or gun hunter. By Larry Smail.

I have always had mixed emotions about the effectiveness of the rear-end shot, and many hunters will agree it should be avoided. On the other hand, there are many experienced hunters who will take this shot, hunting with bow or gun, and there are times when it can be quite deadly, especially at close range. I have seen arrow shots that were driven up the anal opening and completely destroyed everything all the way to the front of the chest cavity. Just as important, when the heavy muscle area of the hip is damaged, it can put a whitetail in a big heap of trouble. But then again, there are times when a hip shot should not be taken. I will discuss more about the hip shot later.

The broadside shot is near-perfect and offers easy access to the lungs for bow or gun hunter. Probably there are only two stipulations regarding the broadside shot. One is that you have to be sure not to hit too far back, as the bullet or arrow must stay forward in order to hit the vitals. The other objective is to be sure the front leg is forward. If the leg is back, the shoulder guards more of the lung area. Bow hunters will find this more of a problem than the gun hunter. The shoulder blade, hit in the right place, can sometimes stop an arrow in its tracks, preventing further penetration.

If the bow hunter is shooting from a tree stand, the shoulder blade becomes even more of a factor, and, it becomes important to hit the deer behind instead of on the shoulder. Close range here is a large factor. The closer the deer is to your stand position, the less area you have to shoot. Whenever I am perched in a tree I would much rather have a whitetail standing 15 yards away as opposed to five yards, and the factor of a high hit is also possible. Even though the arrow is angling downward towards the lungs, there is always a chance that it may not get that far. A whitetail seems to get tougher the higher up on the back you go.

I will always take the broadside shot whenever it is offered, with gun or bow. It just seems to be the kind of a shot you've hoped and waited for.

No one can argue against the angling away shot as the most perfect one, and I would gladly trade 10 quartering-into shots for one quartering away. The reason is simple. There are two places a bullet or arrow could enter and still head all the way downtown.

The angling away shot offers considerably more margin for error than any other shot. You can enter just behind the shoulder and hit the vitals, or hit just in front of the hip and still angle towards the prime area. The latter entry would even take the liver while en route towards the chest cavity.

The angling away shot, when taken from a tree stand, may not be quite as easy as the ground shot. Once again, when shooting from an elevation, you have to hit slightly lower to be sure you are under the spine.

I think it is important not to shy away from the walking shot, even with a bow. You just have to use common sense and allow for the movement. As a whitetail progresses, its front leg is committed to go forward. Time yourself to release the arrow when the leg comes back, then the arrow will most likely hit when the leg is forward. Another advantage to a walking deer is the noise that it makes moving, which can be used to your advantage.

I have never been one to take many running shots at whitetails, but I have done this on occasion and managed to luck out.

Figure 8
Definitely the perfect shot. This shot also allows for a greater margin of error and still reaches the vitals. By Larry Smail.

A running shot is a tough one, and timing is an important factor.
Photo by Leonard Lee Rue III.

I was so surprised when the buck dropped in its tracks that I almost fell out of my tree.

I never attempt this with a bow unless the deer is extremely close and not traveling at superb speed. The main thing a hunter has to do is practice timing his release. Since most of us don't practice releasing on moving targets, we can only consider ourselves fortunate if we manage to do this on a live animal and are successful.

The point is, why take risky, unwarranted shots? Running deer at long range are downright hard to hit, especially in the right places. Long range shots are difficult on a standing white-tail, much less a running one. I'm not saying that you should never attempt a running shot, but take only the ones that offer the best possibilities.

Something that many bow hunters tend to overlook is how height affects the angle of entry. I am basically a full time tree stand hunter, whether with bow or gun. There is not much disadvantage in height angle affecting the gun hunter, but it can certainly affect the shot angle for the bow hunter.

I once climbed to a height of 15 feet and shot an arrow at a particular target. Then I climbed to a height of 22 feet and shot another arrow at the same target. The angle was much steeper from the shot taken at 22 feet.

When the target becomes a whitetail, your shot placement will be affected the same way. The higher up you go, the less target you will have to shoot at. The shot taken from extremely high perches can easily cause you to miss, especially if the dear is close to your stand.

My preferred height when bow hunting is about 16 feet, although, there are times, especially in areas where hunting pressure is heavy, that I may resort to slightly higher altitudes. Decide for yourself, according to the area in which you hunt.

As I mentioned before, shot placement is very important, but it is mainly your own ability that really matters. You must know what you are or are not capable of doing. Anyone who doesn't practice this policy and continues to take shots beyond his capability will continue to miss deer and wound a great many more.

Many deer hunters don't realize a mistaken decision in shooting until it is too late. I have wounded my share of game and made a few mistakes at one time or another. But through mistakes we learn to succeed and cut down on the number of crippled deer. We must be confident that we can make a clean and humane kill when we pull the trigger or release an arrow. This is a factor that can be detrimental to our sport if we do not practice it.

CHAPTER 2

THE BULLET VS.
THE BROADHEAD

I was introduced to the game of bow hunting some 25 years ago, and those days will most likely be in my mind forever. Those were the days before tree blinds had become popular, at least in my neck of the woods.

I suffered ups and downs, like many other beginning hunters. My home state had a bucks only archery season, and things were definitely tough. It was a thrill just to see deer. Getting one seemed almost impossible, and few hunters in the state ever did.

My first hunt came on a bitter cold October morning, one of those days when your feet numb quickly if you spend your time standing, which was exactly what I was doing. My dad placed me behind a large rock to watch over a deer trail about 15 yards from the base, and pointed out which direction the deer would most likely come from. Lo and behold, 30 minutes after dawn, a small buck came down the trail. I could have sworn it would be the biggest buck I would ever see as long as I lived. The buck poked along like it didn't have a care in the world. As I anxiously waited for it to hit an opening, I had a feeling come over me that only a deer hunter can understand. "Buck fever" is a temporary disease most deer hunters experience now and then.

Needless to say the buck quickly put on the brakes and departed in the opposite direction. Obviously the shakes had cost me a possible chance at a buck, or did they? From that moment I was hooked on deer hunting, really hooked. That morning I fell in love with deer hunting, and it became an obsession.

Now the buck fever didn't stop there. For the next couple of years I continued to have problems, only worse. Even though does weren't legal game, I managed to catch the fever. I couldn't stand one of those blasted does coming toward me with a couple of fawns close behind. It seemed they could pick me out every time, without fail. I figured them to be smarter than any buck I would ever encounter. I was hooked, really hooked.

Three years after my bow hunting began I participated in my first gun season. This was ideal since my home state of Indiana permitted a hunter to take a deer with bow or gun. I would have hunted them any legal way, another opportunity to be in the woods. From then on I became a two-season hunter, using bow and gun.

I believe the best education for a beginning gun hunter is to bow hunt first. You learn far beyond what another hunter might teach you as you see deer close up. This will require patience—something all deer hunters must have to be success-ful. It will teach you more about shot placement, to take shots that are not risky or unwarranted. The lessons learned while bow hunting will be applied when you are gun hunting.

Another advantage to bow hunting first is that after seeing several deer, you find yourself more calm and relaxed as the gun season progresses. The anticipation is still there, but enough of the excitement is gone so that you feel at ease when deer come your way. Another nice thing about bow hunting is that it gives you a chance to hunt without wearing all that orange clothing. I don't knock the idea of wearing orange in gun season, but it is nice during bow season to be able to leave your orange hat at home.

I have found that some of my favorite bow season tree stands also produce well during the gun season. It's great to keep on hunting from the same position where you have seen a particular buck all bow season, just out of range, or maybe there was a tree in the way. As the gun season opens, watch out Mr. Buck!

There are many advantages the gun hunter will have over the bow hunter. When a gun hunter shoots, he has a quick option to shoot again, if necessary. I admit that the second or third shot has helped me more than once.

Several years ago, on Thanksgiving morning, I had that kind of luck. The first two hours had been a total lull. Only the presence of an occasional squirrel kept me from climbing out of my stand, so when a doe and fawn came into view I was really surprised. I slowly rose from a sitting position, picked up my gun, and watched intently as the two deer passed, hoping a buck would soon follow. It took nearly 10 nimutes, but finally I heard the crunching of frozen leaves and knew a buck was on the way. It came into view about 60 yards from my stand, its nose glued to the ground, no doubt trailing the doe.

As it reached a small opening I squeezed the trigger, expecting to see the buck drop, but it turned straight away with tail flagging. I was so shocked with the miss that I didn't even get off a second shot. I heard the buck run a short distance, then halt. After a short pause, it started back, slow and cautious, returned to the trail, turned broadside and began following the doe. Not one to look a gift horse in the mouth, I wasted no time in drawing down the bead.

That was one moment only a gun hunter could really understand and appreciate. But the bow hunter also gets those second and third chances. There have been a few times when a second bow shot has helped me. Very few deer shot at with a gun leave and come back, but with a bow this is not uncommon. Many deer aren't spooked by the twang of a bowstring or an arrow buzzing by.

Another gun season disadvantage is having to put up with road hunters. In many areas, including my own, this is a real problem. Many guys use extreme cold temperatures as an excuse to hunt by using vehicles instead of legs, guys who own deer tags and merely try to fill them in this manner. During the archery season this is usually not a problem.

Now let's consider mixing bow and gun hunting during the same season. Some states have bow season overlapping the gun season, and special hunts may allow either bow or gun. I have found the latter a real challenge for the bow hunter.

A few years ago I participated in a special drawing hunt on a wildlife refuge in Southern Indiana, to include 75 muzzle loading and 75 bow hunters. Since I was using a bow, I was not overly enthusiastic. It was a prime area with big bucks almost anywhere, but since gun hunters were possible on both sides, I took the hunt pretty calmly.

Just after daylight guns started popping from every direction. I saw a few deer, but nothing seemed to come close. I worried about hitting a deer and losing it to a gun hunter somewhere ahead. About 9:30 a bunch of 23 deer came by in single file, following a small creek. An extremely large doe worked its way within 20 yards of my stand and I released an arrow. The hit was too far back and I spent the next two hours trailing, expecting to run into a gut pile along the way. I was really pleased when I found the doe. I hadn't expected to kill a deer that day, and it field dressed at 142 pounds, the biggest doe I had ever taken.

The possibility is always there of another hunter shooting or finding your deer before you get to it. The risk is not as great during archery season, but it has happened. The gun hunter has this worry, expecially in areas where pressure is great.

I really enjoyed myself during the 1983 gun season in Indiana. For the first four mornings I had seen deer, a bunch of does traveling a hillside across a hollow from my stand. Each morning the same buck chased them, and each day I cursed myself for not having moved my stand to that hillside. On the fifth morning I figured my luck had changed, as the buck chased the does across the hollow to the lower edge of the hill that I was perched on. I wanted this buck for many reasons. It was nice, not a whopper, but decent, and sported a unique right antler. However, my main reason was because I had to sit and watch it every morning, just out of range.

As it crossed the hollow and turned broadside, I shot and it went down and thrashed violently. I shucked the empty shell and got ready in case a second shot was needed. The buck had fallen behind a blowdown, and its neck and head were going up and down. After watching for a couple of minutes, I assumed it must be spine shot and couldn't get up. Since there was no chance for a second shot from my tree blind, I elected to climb down and finish off the old boy.

I heard a commotion when about half way down the tree, turned to see it was almost on its feet and trying desperately to get going. By the time I reached the ground the buck was up and moving away, offering no chance at another shot. Since I was in an area with several other hunters around, I decided to follow immediately.

I easily found blood and started trailing. Every time I rounded a bend, I hoped to see it. After five minutes I heard a loud boom ahead, felt another hunter had possibly shot the buck, but decided to stay on the blood trail. After a few more minutes I came up on the stone dead buck. A hunter standing over him informed me the buck had come up the draw just before he shot, and didn't have any idea it had already been hit until I arrived. We found two wounds, my shot just in front of the shoulder where the neck joins, and his behind the ear, no doubt dropping the buck in its tracks. I shrugged it off and went home, deciding to call it a day.

As I mentioned in Chapter 1, it is vital to know how the broadhead kills and how the bullet kills. The broadhead severs and causes hemorrhaging, and cuts a slice up to one and a half inches or wider, depending on its size. The bullet mutilates and explodes, causing a great amount of shock. Both are deadly and can do great damage.

I once ran into a gun hunter who tried to convince me that bow hunting should be outlawed. He said he found a dead buck with seven arrows in it. I merely laughed and told him that was impossible. The guy was hard nosed and obviously couldn't have known what he was talking about. The point is, some hunters don't understand how effective a razor sharp broadhead can be. The dull broadhead, on the other hand, will merely push its way into the deer and shove tissue or even arteries out of the way, without much cutting. Every bow hunter as a top priority should use only razor sharp broadheads.

The shocking power of a bullet can do great damage. Possibly the buck I just wrote about was in temporary shock. I have seen gun hits that knocked whitetails down and left them in shock, while others merely ran off like nothing happened, even after being hit in the vitals. Of course, they didn't keep running long.

Any serious wound can put a whitetail in shock, even with an arrow hit. When hunting in Pennsylvania some 15 years ago, I took a risky shot at a nice buck which had come into a clover field and never attempted to come closer. With darkness fast approaching, knowing I might never see the buck again, I chanced a 40 yard shot.

I knew when the arrow hit it was too far back and somewhat high. The buck actually staggered back into the woods, out of visibility. After a 30 minute wait I headed for the woods with my light in hopes of recovering the deer. An excellent blood trail led me directly to the still alive buck, which rolled its eyes back and forth, slowly came to its feet, staggered around and slowly walked off with lowered head. I carefully marked the spot and left the woods, assuming I could come back the next morning to find the buck.

When I again picked up the trail the blood seemed to go back and forth, indicating that the buck was still staggering. After about 100 yards the trail finally straightened out, then for the next 100 yards went perfectly straight and led me to two beds the buck had laid in. There was positively no blood trail after the second bed, and although I spent the rest of the day looking for the buck, it was fruitless.

This buck had probably gone into shock shortly after being wounded, and stayed that way until the point where the trail straightened out. I feel certain that it recovered and lived long enough to end up on a wall other than my own.

I have encountered other bow and gun hits where shock was a factor. I have learned that if this happens in the morning, a hunter can take advantage of the situation and dispose of the animal while he still has daylight to work with.

A hunter should know what to expect when trailing a whitetail shot by an arrow or a gun. Very few gun hits will bleed as quickly as the arrow-shot deer. Many times I have found the bullet wound will not bleed for a great distance, even in the vitals. Many gun hunters think they missed just because no blood was visible where the animal was shot. An arrow wound through the vitals, however, will usually begin bleeding within 20 yards of the shot.

Anyone who hunts should know a bullet wound blood trail is very sparse, even after the trailing has begun. I have seen few gun hits that bled as well as most arrow hits. This makes the gun hunter realize he has a very important responsibility to know for sure whether or not a hit was made.

A whitetail shot through the vitals with an arrow will usually die as quickly as with a gun hit through the vitals. Some hunters may be more impressed with the gun hit, solely because of the knockdown power. It is impressive when a shot knocks a deer to the ground, but the broadhead is just as effective.

There are times when a whitetail hit by an arrow will bed down close to the spot where it was shot. There was no loud blast to scare the animal and no knocking power to rile it up. If unaware of sudden danger, it will try to ease itself by bedding down quickly. This gives the hunter the opportunity to stay put and not push the animal further away.

Most bow hunters are aware that an arrow can make a glancing hit under certain conditions. Usually when a deer is quartering into the hunter it will glance, particularly when it hits the shoulder blade. I have seen arrows slide along the shoulder and not penetrate until they hit the soft paunch area. I have also seen arrows slide down a rib and off the deer without any penetration. This will happen at extremely close yardage from an elevated position.

Few gun hunters are aware that a bullet can slide along a bone, just as the broadhead can do. One particular whitetail I shot at about 30 yards as it was quartering into and almost facing me. Fortunately, my second shot caught it square before it managed to escape. Upon close examination I found the first bullet had merely grazed the shoulder blade and the right side of the body, never penetrating.

A question sometimes asked is, "can someone tell when a deer has been shot by an arrow or a bullet?" The answer is a definite yes. Many conservation officers are trained to tell, and many experienced hunters can also tell. When looking at a broadhead hole, the hide is neatly sliced and you can almost put the hide back to a closing point if pushing from the inside out. The bullet hole actually mutilates its entry, while the exit hole is very jagged with no perfect form.

Some of us will always be gun hunters, some just bow hunters, and some like to do it any way. We can choose to hunt with any weapon we want, as long as it is legal. The main thing is to know the limitations. That is your responsibility.

Those who do not bow hunt because of a lack of confidence in the broadhead are totally missing out. I will always be a two season hunter because it is another reason to go after the white-tail. I know the damage a broadhead can do when placed in the right spot, and I am fully aware of its capabilities and potential.

All in all, I have probably enjoyed bow kills more than gun kills, but both experiences have been very rewarding. I still realize a great feeling of accomplishment whether I have succeeded with gun or bow.

CHAPTER 3

AFTER THE SHOT

*T*he buck slowly made its way up the wooded draw toward the bow hunter's tree stand. The hunter watched him for several minutes. The buck stopped only 30 yards from the hidden hunter's position to scent the air current. Once again it started walking, still on a crash course with the hunter.

As the buck reached a tree the bow hunter had marked as his 20 yard spot, it turned slightly to the right and exposed the rib cage. The hunter wasted no time in coming to full draw. Quickly he brought his preferred sight pin down to a spot only a couple of inches behind the buck's shoulder. The buck still continued a slow walk, helping the hunter get perfect timing. When it seemed like now or never the hunter released his arrow. Instantly the buck bolted, bore to its left and was gone, so fast it was like he had never been there.

The bow hunter silently scratched his head and wondered what had happened. Had he hit the deer? If he had, in which direction did the deer go? Was there blood on the ground only a few yards from his stand? If he did hit the deer, exactly where did his arrow hit? Did the deer appear wounded? Should he climb down out of his stand now, or should he wait?

These types of questions are usually going through a deer hunter's mind after he has shot. Probable answers may be vital to the hunter's chance of recovery, if a hit was indeed made. So many times a hunter is left wondering what really happened.

At the time the shot is taken a hunter is excited. After all, this was the moment he waited for. The excitement clouds what actually happened, and the hunter is left speculating.

We have to know how to make the best of things when a shot has been fired. We have to recognize each event that took place until the whitetail vanished, then we will better know what to do next. How you handle yourself after a shot may very well determine how you may spend the next several hours.

Probably one of the first things a deer hunter should do is take notice of a whitetail's reactions when shot at. The bow hunter and the gun hunter will witness different responses. Basically, we try to determine whether or not a hit has been made.

I have never personally seen a whitetail that stuck around after being hit through the body cavity, with bow or gun, provided it was not spine shot. I have slightly grazed whitetails with an arrow, had them run a few yards and then stop. Sometimes they even blow at me and continue to walk off as though nothing happened. I have heard stories about deer hit through the body cavity which run, then stop and snort. I can't verify this since I have never had it happen.

One situation I read about told of a bow hunter walking along a picked corn field to his stand one afternoon when a small buck came out of a pine thicket and began feeding. After a 15 minute stalk, the hunter was able to sneak up within 50 yards of the occupied deer, standing broadside. He decided to shoot, released the arrow and thought it looked good. The buck threw his head up quickly, stared in the direction of the hunter, then put his head down and went back to feeding. Assuming he missed, the hunter removed another arrow from his quiver to try a second shot. At that moment the buck dropped to its knees, rolled on its side and after a few kicks, lay motionless.

The hunter, not believing what he had seen, slowly approached the downed buck, which was quite dead. The arrow had hit the buck through the chest cavity, just behind the shoulders, a good lung shot.

Although I can't verify this, it is another of those strange cases we hear about, and are left to wonder.

Any deer I have ever hit in the vitals, bow or gun, has always left at breakneck speed, then usually gone into a hard run. This seems to be the most common reaction. As a matter of fact, almost every whitetail I have shot through the body cavity, other than the paunch shot, has left like a racehorse.

Usually they run so hard that their bellies are very low to the ground. Generally they run right over the top of obstacles. I have seen them go through the middle of log jams or over a briar patch, running for their lives.

No one can say what goes through a whitetail's mind at a moment like this, but evidently there must be a great fear. I don't really believe they think about it, but I do believe instinct tells them that survival is at stake.

Another noticeable thing the whitetail does when hit is to drop its tail. In cases where the deer is standing with the tail already down, it leaves without bringing the tail up. How often do you see whitetails run without flagging? Not often, unless the deer is hit.

The tucked tail is a general rule of thumb, not always so, but true most of the time. If you shoot at a whitetail and it leaves quickly with its tail tucked, I'll bet it has been hit. If the deer leaves at a slower run, with the tail flagging, most likely it was not hit. This is not the case all the time, but odds are a deer will react in this manner.

Most gun hunters usually think that when a deer is shot at, it will quickly leave the area, whether hit or not. This is not true. The loud blast may sometimes frighten it, but not always. This seems to be a sound that some whitetails have adjusted to.

I recall one evening many years ago when I was perched up about 20 feet in a white oak tree, overlooking an area of thickets. A slight hill was a little west of me, about 90 yards away. I first

When the deer you have shot at suddenly breaks away from the others, there is a good possibility the deer has been hit. Photo by Irene Vandermolen.

noticed a single deer silhouetted on top of the hill. Since the state I was hunting in allowed shotgun slugs only, I was using my favorite deer slug gun with open sights. With binoculars I checked out a nice doe, but since the law was antlered deer only, I just watched as she picked her way along. I then saw a smaller doe come to the top of the hill, and presumed it most likely a fawn of that year. Soon a small buck came into view.

Sighted for 60 yards, I knew in order to take the buck I would have to be on just perfect. I rested the gun against the oak and aimed a little higher than normal. I squeezed off the shot, but the buck just stood there and didn't flinch a muscle. Before I squeezed off a second shot, another deer popped over the hill and its rack showed up easily at 90 yards. I rested the gun again and took another shot, but all four deer stayed perfectly still. I took another shot, missed again, and the large buck turned away to look in the opposite direction. It was obvious none of these deer were spooked by the noise of the shotgun or the whizzing slugs.

The large buck walked over the hill and out of view, so my attention switched back to the smaller buck. The shotgun roared and it jumped straight up in the air and took off at a fast speed. The other deer, seeing the smaller buck flee, did the same.

The small buck was indeed hit, but up until that time the four shots did not bother him or the other deer. Most likely they would still be standing there if I hadn't hit the smaller buck. It is the deer's reaction that will usually tell you whether you have missed or not.

I have also hit a few deer that managed to run off with several others before finally breaking away on a direction of their own. This is a good way to tell if you have hit a particular deer. When all take off running, watch to see if one in particular breaks away from the others. If so, there is a good possibility it is the one that you shot at, most likely wounded. This can be the case whether you are hunting with gun or bow.

The most convincing moment a gun hunter will have is when he shoots and the deer drops immediately. This is one way of knowing you have hit the deer, but not always. I remember a couple of occasions when I had deer stumble and practically fall, even though I had missed. This is a rare circumstance, but when your gun fires and scares them, they leave so quickly that they lose their footing in the process.

Like most gun hunters, I love to see a deer drop in its tracks as soon as I shoot. We usually start patting ourselves on the back for a job well done. I have seen some whitetails literally knocked off their feet, while others just dropped to their knees, then to the ground.

The bullet, with enough force behind it, produces a lot of power. To a whitetail it is like a big thrust suddenly hitting it. When a deer is shot through both shoulders, it will usually drop, but not always. This just seems to be the kind of a hit that drops them the quickest.

I have shot whitetails through the shoulders and had them merely run off, showing no sign of being hit. This is more common in a paunch shot than a shoulder shot, but it does happen now and then. It pays not to jump to conclusions and think you have missed just because a deer didn't respond the way you assume it should.

Make every effort to check a whitetail's trail after you have shot, whether or not you think you missed. There is always a possibility that your shot was more on target than you believed.

Many bow hunters are actually able to hear the arrow-whitetail contact. This depends on how close the deer is and exactly where in the body it is hit. Usually, from 15 to 30 yards, I will be fortunate enough to hear the arrow hit.

Any arrow that hits the chest area or paunch section will produce a very dull "thump" sound. An arrow that hits bone, such as the shoulder blade or a leg bone, will sound more like a loud crack. When an arrow hits the ribs the sound is still dull, because soft rib bones break easily.

There is no bigger disappointment than a bow hunter who finds his arrow lodged solid in a tree trunk. Sometimes the case.

An important step is to remember where the deer was standing when the shot was made. A particular tree or bush may give you that exact spot.

Most deer, when taking off quickly after being shot at, are almost certain to kick up dirt and leaves at the spot they were standing. This can be so important when it comes time to look for it or blood. The hunter who has snow on the ground has a great advantage and should easily find where the deer was standing.

The hunter in a tree stand should have a much better view than the ground hunter, and easily pick out a landmark as the deer goes past. The ground hunter should try to pick out a landmark and notice the direction the deer takes. Rocks, trees, creeks, and bushes all serve as pinpoint locations, if you can pick them out. You will find that remembering such landmarks will enable you to find your blood trail much quicker than just knowing a general direction.

The hunter who shoots in the morning has all day to find a blood trail, if necessary, but the hunter who shoots late may end up looking for his sign in the dark, or the last few minutes of the evening when visibility is poorest.

I once had a bow hunter call me up, just after I arrived home from an evening's hunt, to help him trail a deer he was certain he had hit. When we arrived at his stand, it was about as dark as dark can get. He had no markers out and had never found a beginning blood trail. I assured the hunter that we would eventually find the trail if he could show me the direction the deer had taken. I spent the next hour looking but found nothing. The hunter was sure of his direction, so rather than argue that he might be wrong, I suggested we wait until morning and try again.

Just after daylight I started looking in the direction the hunter had shown me the evening before. Finding nothing, I asked if he could be wrong about the direction and suggested he climb into his tree stand and look at it from up there.

Sure enough, once in the tree he began to see things differently and suggested I look for blood about 75 yards north of the original direction. Within minutes we had a trail that almost anyone could have followed and after 90 yards we were field dressing one of the biggest four point racks I had ever seen.

Any hunter can become confused when looking over an area from a tree stand, then climbing down. Things have a tendency to change when you reach ground level. That is why it is important to pick a landmark, one you can easily spot out of your stand.

As soon as you find where the deer was standing, mark the spot with white or other bright colored toilet paper. Tie it around a limb about head high, easily noticeable at great distances, even in thick cover. Use a large amount for a flag as nothing shows up day or night better than bright colored toilet paper. Always carry it with you (you should anyway). The nice thing is that rain will decompose it almost completely.

I have seen many bow hunters mark a blood trail, or a spot where a deer was shot at, with an arrow, sometimes hard to see even in daylight, much less at night. I have also seen hunting caps, hunting jackets, guns, bows, you name it, as markers. I guess any marker is better than none.

One sign of a whitetail being hit is when it runs hard with the tail tucked.
Photo by Leonard Lee Rue Jr.

If you don't have toilet paper, scraping a bare spot on the woods floor serves as a good marker, but do not scrape back leaves that may have blood on them. I have used this method when trailing alone for long distances, and can easily back trail if necessary.

Another useful item is a compass. Many hunters carry one as a regular practice, but few use them to take readings. Whether in a tree stand or on the ground, a compass reading should be taken of the direction the deer took. This will give you a precise bearing on the wounded deer and may come in handy, especially if you leave to get trailing help.

One big question after a shot is how long until beginning trailing. The waiting game will be more fully discussed in another chapter, noting the possibilities of waiting or pushing game. These details will help the hunter to understand what may or may not happen as a result of waiting.

The tree stand hunter wonders how long to stay before climbing down, which brings us back to waiting. A hunter should remain in his stand at least 15 to 20 minutes, providing the animal has not bedded down within view. If the deer has bedded close by, stay put and watch it closely.

A certain amount of disturbance is made climbing out of a tree, so try to get down as quietly as possible. There's nothing worse than a hunter banging his way down, stepping into a pile of dry leaves, and making things sound like the Fourth of July.

If you have waited 20 minutes before climbing down, there is still a chance to pursue a deer quickly, if it is a hit that requires pushing the animal in order to have a better chance of recovery. This is the case on some hits, so it is important to know the opportunity will still be there.

Other situations may be enough to alter how long to stay in a tree. If there is a great deal of gun hunting pressure I suggest you consider trailing at once to prevent another hunter from shooting your deer before you get to it. Of course, once again the type of hit you have made should be taken into consideration.

If you have paunched or liver shot a deer, and it has bedded close by, immediate trailing may only push it to another hunter. Probably your best bet on a shot in that area of the body cavity would be to leave it alone. Following chapters will help you understand the pros and cons of immediate or prolonged trailing.

Experience is your best guide. Over the years I have made wrong decisions, but I learned from my mistakes.

Once you have found where the deer was standing when you shot, it is important to know what to look for. The first thing a hunter looks for is blood, but most of the time there will be none at the location where the deer was hit. Wounded deer rarely bleed until they have traveled a short distance. I have seen some artery hits bleed immediately, usually from arrow wounds.

On a few occasions I have seen a gun hit deer bleed instantly. One whitetail was shot through the front of the shoulder where it joins the front legs, actually more of a scrape wound. When a whitetail drops to the ground after being shot,

it may leave blood at that location. Usually it takes a few seconds to get back on its feet, allowing time for bleeding to begin.

The bow hunter will try to find an arrow to inform him of
a pass-through and what type of hit. Many arrows are hard to
find in woods or thickets, especially if the shot came from
ground level when the arrow tends to slide under everything.
The tree stand hunter should find the arrow somewhat easier,
especially if shot at close yardage, but sometimes even these are
hard to locate. Many times you hope you don't find your arrow,
a sign that the whitetail may have left with it.

Many chapters will discuss how soon a whitetail will start
bleeding upon a certain type of hit, as each reacts differently and
should be discussed individually.

When I was bow hunting on a special quota deer hunt at
Land Between The Lakes, on the Kentucky side, many years
ago, I learned the real meaning of arrow disappointment. I had
seen a lot of deer on a two day hunt, but nothing ventured into
shooting range. On the last evening I had a fallow deer working
its way to my stand. It was legal game and my Kentucky tag
would have no use after that evening, so I was praying the deer
would come into range. Slowly but surely it worked its way to
within 20 yards of my stand and turned broadside. I knew it was
going to be easy and was relaxed when I came to full draw.
When I released my arrow, the fallow let out a little bark,
jumped about a foot off the ground, and took off like a bat out
of you know where. The deer jumped into a large brush pile
about 60 yards from me and all was quiet.

I sat down to give it a few minutes and prematurely started
to congratulate myself for I just knew I had killed my first
fallow deer. After a few minutes I walked the direction the deer
had taken. Even though I saw no blood, I wasn't worried. I just
knew the deer was in the middle of the brush pile. I looked in
from every angle, but could see no deer. After crawling around
for another 10 minutes, I started to become concerned.

I went back to where I had shot the deer, figured I would
just pick up the blood trail and do this by the book. I noticed my
arrow sticking out of the ground and snatched it up to look at

that crimson stain from one end to the other. Trouble was, there wasn't any blood to be found. I had missed, and looked around to be sure nobody had witnessed this embarrassing incident. So much for what I thought was an easy kill.

Hair is sometimes found at the location of the hit and is also found on an arrow shaft. This can tell a great deal as to where in the body the deer has been hit, to be discussed in the following chapter.

Many chapters will describe how soon a whitetail will start bleeding upon a certain type of hit. All types bleed differently, therefore we must look at each according to its body location.

It is important to keep as calm as possible after a shot. I know this is difficult because I have been through it many times. To help improve chances of recovering a wounded whitetail, take notice of everything that follows the shot. Sometimes it is the information gained here that will help down the trail.

Photo of the author's son.

CHAPTER 4

THE SIGNIFICANCE OF DEER HAIR

*E*ach year the whitetail changes color as its hair is shed or thickened. In the summer it appears with a reddish shade, and during the winter months has a brilliant grayish cast. The time of year for change depends upon the northern or southern latitude, and physical condition may also play a role.

The winter coat will be shed in the spring, and many times a person will find shedded hairs. When turkey hunting during April and May in my home state of Indiana, I have found large bunches in one clump, then a little further down the trail another clump.

The deer hunter should mainly be concerned with the winter coat. Many times you can spot whitetails just beginning to change to a winter coat in early to late fall. Some I see in November are still reddish in spots while others are already gray.

The winter hair is actually hollow and filled with air to make far better insulation against the cold and keep the deer somewhat waterproof. The winter coats farther north have darker coats than those of the south. The whitetail's winter hair is, basically, dark gray and grayish-brown at the tip.

51

It is important for the hunter to know what color hair comes from what part of the body. The color and thickness does change slightly at different points of the body. Certain areas contain white hair. There are whitish areas around the eyes, around the muzzle, inside the ears, a throat patch, rump and belly, down the inside of each leg, and of course, on the underneath side of the tail.

Several years ago a hunter who had just come out from a morning's hunt advised me that there was a white deer in the area. Since I have always enjoyed seeing a few of these beauties, I asked where. He said he did not see the deer, but had found white hair on a barbed wire fence.

Probably the poor guy is now aware of how foolish he must have sounded, and hopefully he has learned that all whitetails have some white hair.

All deer hunters should familiarize themselves with the winter coat. Many times hair will be the only thing found when you have shot a deer. Usually hair is found where a deer is shot. I seldom find hair when trailing a wounded deer, but have found that hair was the only clue that I hit the whitetail.

An arrow slices off hair as soon as it enters a deer's hide, and if it is a pass-through, the hunter will find hair on his broadhead and arrow shaft. Whether a pass-through or not, there is bound to be a few hairs, but don't expect to find a large amount. If you find a large glob of hair, more than likely your arrow ran along the side of the deer. This usually cuts off large amounts and hair is easily found if you're looking in the right place.

One of the most intriguing trailing jobs I have ever been on was due to finding a large amount of hair on the ground. My friend shot a doe while it was bedded down a short distance from his tree stand. The arrow had evidently sliced the deer for several inches along the body. A lot of hair was found and a blind man could almost have followed the blood trail, which we found for better than a mile in the dark before we were forced to give it up. We never located this deer, but when I look back I wish we had pursued it more that night. Had we continued to slowly push the doe and keep it moving, we might have sooner or later caused enough blood loss so it would have gone down. It was one of those hits you could swear severed an artery.

I personally keep a buck's winter coat hanging on the wall, for inspection of hair I find from wounded whitetails. It comes in handy to compare the sample hair to the rug hair. Be sure to keep one hanging on the wall, not on the floor, since a winter coat of hollow hair is very brittle and breaks off easily. A deer hide on the floor won't last long. Keep your tanned hide out of the sun, also as it will bleach out very quickly.

The gun hunter also has a good chance of finding hair at the exact shot location. He will find more hair from a graze shot than a direct punch through, but even the direct hit will knock hair off. Many times when blood is not available, and this is often the case with a bullet wound, deer hair may be all you get to tip off the wound's whereabouts.

This has helped me on two occasions, but one incident in particular stands out in my mind. It was the third day of Indiana's gun season and I was in a tree stand overlooking a line of scrapes I had hunted the previous bow season without much luck. About an hour before dark the wind picked up and a cold front started moving in. I wasn't prepared for the weather, but persisted to stay in the tree.

About 30 minutes before dark I glimpsed movement to my left. Since the wind was blowing hard, hearing was nearly impossible. Since I could not see it plainly moving through the thickets, I didn't reach for my gun hanging on a limb. The buck popped out into the open only 20 yards from my stand. As I slowly reached for my gun, the buck threw its head up and stared at me for what seemed like 15 minutes. Finally it lowered its head back to level ground, evidently content that I was nothing. I slowly inched the gun to my shoulder and buried my open sights on its left front shoulder, angled slightly to me. I really didn't want to shoot, but it continued to stay put, feeling certain things weren't just right. I squeezed off the trigger, the shotgun slug roared toward its destination, but the buck turned and loped away showing absolutely no sign of being hit.

At first I couldn't believe my eyes. Had I really missed at only 20 yards? As I sat in my stand with darkness fast approaching, impatience got the best of me and I climbed down to find nothing where the deer had taken off. I searched in the direction the buck had gone for 30 minutes but never found blood. Finally, with my flashlight on, I went back to the spot where the buck had been standing and got down on my hands and knees. I found about a half dozen hairs, convincing me of a hit. At home I was able to identify the hair as coming from the shoulder area, predicting a possible good hit.

The next morning I crawled on hands and knees for better than an hour but could find no sign of blood. I finally gave up and began concentrating on finding the deer. A deer hit through the shoulder shouldn't go far. I followed the direction the buck had taken and within 70 yards found the seven pointer.

I was lucky to find this buck, maybe not that I found it, but fortunate to find the hair. Without it I might have assumed a miss and the buck could have wasted away. Never take for granted that you have missed. Always check until there is no doubt left in your mind.

The importance of knowing deer hair cannot be overemphasized. It can help determine that you have made a hit, and also where.

There is usually no way to tell by the hair which might represent entry and which might determine exit. Sometimes you can attempt to piece that together, if you are sure of the deer's angle when it was shot. You might be able to determine which comes from where, particularly if you are fortunate to find hair from two different body locations.

If you are in woods and have plenty of leaves available where you hit, pick them up individually and carefully turn them over. You will be surprised how much easier it is to see hair instead of just looking over a large portion of leaves at once. Be sure to get on your hands and knees when looking for hair. If you are standing, or even slightly bent over, you will probably never see any.

An Identification Guide to Deer Hair

1. Stomach or Side Hair—very coarse, hollow, brownish gray, medium length, tips not dark as they are higher up on the deer.

2. Navel Hair—all white and very coarse. Also hollow. Will appear curly and twisted, very long.

3. Spine Hair—very coarse, hollow, long dark gray hair with black tips.

4. Top of Back Hair—very coarse, hollow, long dark gray hair with black tips, shorter than spine hair.

5. Ham Hair—very coarse, medium length, not as long as chest hair, dark gray with dark tips.

6. Lower Leg Hair—coarse, medium to short, gray to brown, with dark tips.

7. Hair Between Hind Legs—not hollow, very fine, white and silky, and also curly.

8. Heart and Lung Hair—very coarse, very long dark hair, with black tips.

9. Brisket—very coarse, long and dark gray, with dark tips, very stiff, but can curl.

10. Neck Hair—dark gray and short, front of neck will be light gray to white, also short.

11. Tail Hair—very long, top hair is dark and wavy, tipped in black. Underneath is white and also wavy.

Deer hair is just as important as a blood trail, so take as much interest in finding it as you do blood. There are times when I know I made a good hit, and couldn't care less about a few hairs, but other times finding a few hairs may mean filling a deer tag.

CHAPTER 5

ARROW ANALYSIS

*A*lthough this chapter deals mainly with educating the bow hunter, the gun hunter may learn from it as well. Such things as penetration, arrow condition, and blood on the shaft, will give knowledgeable information which may assist in any deer hunter's trailing techniques.

Probably one major controversy among bow hunters is arrow penetration. Does an arrow do more good when left inside of a fleeing whitetail, or does it do more good when shot completely through? In reality, both sides have hard ground to stand on.

When the whitetail carries off an arrow, we wonder what good can it do the bow hunter? If the hit is through the vitals, it won't much matter as the deer is doomed to a quick death. Many hunters feel that when an arrow is left in the body cavity, and only the last few inches of the shaft stick out, the razor sharp broadhead continues to do great damage as the deer bumps the arrow. Usually this is exactly what will happen.

Imagine having the business end of an arrow embedded in you, with someone on the other end moving it back and forth? It makes you cringe to think about it.

As the arrow bumps by a tree, bush, or whatever, it cuts again and again, causing further internal damage. This may cause the deer to hemorrhage sooner than if the arrow had passed through.

Some bow hunters argue that the whitetail which carries off an arrow will offer a better blood trail. They claim that the arrow in the deer is certain to keep the hole open to bleed more freely.

In my opinion, this is only true to a certain extent. I have learned from many bowshot trailing experiences that there is only one type of hit that offers a better blood trail from an arrow staying in the deer. That is the paunch shot deer. When shot completely through, the stomach and intestines clog the hole, making it almost impossible for blood to get to the ground. The held arrow will generally keep the hole from clogging, and if open, blood gets out to the ground much easier.

When we look at a deer shot completely through, we have two holes, not one as when the deer holds in the arrow. This makes for a better trail because there are two holes for blood to leak out, an asset for the gun hunter as well. It is even better if the shot is from a tree stand, the lower exit hole usually resulting in an even better blood trail than the ground level shot.

Another bonus for the pass-through shot is that it penetrates every organ or artery in the arrow's path. You have done great damage and don't have to rely on further harm that might come from a little banging around.

Still another reason for my being partial to a pass-through is that in most cases you are able to find your arrow. This can provide you with deer hair and blood color, which might help determine the type of hit. Many times that is what I needed to reassure me that I would recover a whitetail. By assuming a possible killing shot, we can go ahead with trailing. If an arrow indicates a hit that may require waiting, it is another pass-through advantage. I have trailed many whitetails in both circumstances and always favor the pass-through shot. I firmly believe it is the best you can have.

If you have shot completely through a whitetail, usually your arrow will stick in the ground, especially if you shot from a tree. It should be only a few feet past the spot where the deer was standing. If you have shot through the body cavity, your arrow should be blood covered from end to end. The paunch shot will many times leave a slimy, or even smelly, area on the shaft.

Sometimes tallow is found on the arrow. Hits that cause only tallow to appear on the shaft will be discussed later.

When an arrow is retrieved with blood on only one side of the broadhead and arrow shaft, assume you either shot high or low and grazed the deer. It is heartbreaking to see blood on one side of your arrow, but the other side slick as can be. There are times when a pass-through arrow may wipe clean on wet grass or other obstacles, therefore you should still put forth effort into trailing as far as you possibly can.

I know of one bow hunter who told me of a situation where it seemed he had no hope of recovering a buck he had shot. All the arrow shaft had on it were a few light specks of blood. When he began trailing, blood was splattered all along the side of the trail, and he recovered the buck in less than 100 yards. It had been hit in the neck, evidently through the carotid artery, but the arrow had gone through so much wet honeysuckle that it was wiped almost clean.

Many times a bow hunter finds the tip of the broadhead bent, a result of hitting bone. The shoulder blade, spine or leg bones are good about bending broadhead tips. Since ribs are soft, it is unlikely a broadhead will bend from hitting them. There are times when a bent broadhead may only mean an injured tree or rock.

Sometimes a bow hunter will find his arrow just lying on the ground. Several circumstances may cause this. Even though the arrow is blood soaked, but not sticking, you shot completely through. When a whitetail turns to leave, it may run over or kick your arrow out of the ground. Usually you can find dirt on the broadhead tip, proof the arrow had stuck in.

A couple of years ago my son took a shot at a doe, but apparently missed. I found his arrow several feet past the spot where the deer was standing, sticking straight up out of the ground at a 90 degree angle, completely clean of blood and tallow. However, the nock end was completely covered by white hair. We assumed the deer turned and ran over the arrow, catching the nock end on the underneath side of the belly, and standing the arrow up.

Even though you may have shot through a whitetail, it may stick out of the departure hole, broadhead first. Many times the deer will carry the arrow a short distance before it falls free. How soon the arrow drops depends on where the deer is hit. If heavy muscle is holding the front half, the deer may carry it for a long way before it drops out. If in the paunch, the deer will drop the arrow much sooner, since the area is soft. As the deer runs off, it may sometimes bend the broadhead half of the arrow as it hits obstacles.

If you find your arrow and the front half (nock end) is bent, that is a good sign you didn't shoot all the way through the deer. More than likely you can tell how much of the arrow was in the deer by checking the exact spot of the bend.

If you shoot a 30 inch arrow, and 14 inches down from the nock is where the bend starts, assume you had 16 inches in the deer. This system is not always accurate, but usually it is very close.

As a whitetail runs, sometimes part of the arrow will work its way back out from the entrance hole. You can tell how much arrow was in the deer by checking blood on the shaft. The part that is covered solid all the way around was in the deer. The other portion will probably have splattered blood in spots. When a whitetail runs with an arrow in it, the blood tends to be thrown out somewhat from the arrow's vibrations.

I was fortunate on one occasion to see a whitetail pull an arrow from the wound, and other bow hunters may have witnessed this. A small buck hit in the toughest part of the shoulder ran about 40 yards from my stand, stopped, grabbed with its mouth and flipped the arrow a few feet away. I have heard other bow hunters say they have seen whitetails pull arrows out of their hips.

One evening I shot a doe a little high and too far back, catching it in the loin area. The deer carried the arrow, and after I trailed for a couple hundred yards, found an area about 30 feet in diameter where blood was everywhere. After picking up her trail once again, I found the arrow. I am certain the circle of blood came as the doe tried to pull the arrow.

Many times, when you recover your deer but find no arrow, it is because the deer has flipped the arrow a few feet. Since you are busy looking at the trail, you don't see the arrow when you pass by.

Arrows are many times broken off, leaving the broadhead embedded in the deer, which everyone hates to see happen. I have seen arrows break off in the spine, loin, hip, shoulder, legs and head. Anywhere there is bone or heavy muscle, an arrow can break off.

I had an unusual circumstance soon after I began bow hunting. One morning, perched in a tree just off the edge of a pine thicket, I spotted a deer which walked directly beneath my stand. Since it was the straight-down shot or nothing, I decided to take it. I hit the deer on the left side of the rib cage and knew I was forward, just behind the shoulder. My penetration, however, was only a few inches. After trailing about 150 yards, I lost the blood trail. After another hour of finding nothing, I decided to call it quits. I never retrieved my arrow, and was very disappointed, since I hoped the deer would be my first bow kill.

The following year a good friend was hunting the same stand one evening when a small buck came in. He made a good hit and after a short trailing job, we dressed out a five pointer. After he got the deer home and began skinning it, he found a broadhead and a piece of microflite arrow shaft inside the chest cavity. Sure enough, it was my arrow shaft and broadhead, the type I hunted with the year before.

Since I had hit only one deer the previous year, I knew it had to be the same one, killed from the stand one year later. A membrane had built up around the broadhead and shaft enclosed in the rib cage. The buck had a slightly deformed right antler, but otherwise had evidently healed from its wound with no other problems.

I have heard of other similar cases, but am still amazed at how a whitetail can recover. If no organs are hit, a deer can evidently mend itself from an arrow left inside.

Many arrows are lost each year from misses and I have certainly lost my share. It is a good practice to make every effort to retrieve your arrows when they are shot. Many times bow hunters have suspected a miss and not known otherwise until they found a blood soaked arrow. One hunter I heard about shot at a doe during the morning hours from his tree stand, never found his arrow, and assumed he had missed. When he came back to hunt again in the evening, he found the doe only about 60 yards from his stand.

We can never be too sure about a missed shot, therefore we should put every possible effort into confirming that we did miss. A lot of times the only way to do this is find the arrow.

One Pennsylvania farmer refuses to let anybody hunt on his property because of flattened tractor tires received from arrows left in his field. Under those conditions I certainly sympathize with him.

When we shoot, it is our responsibility to retrieve an arrow. One way to help find aluminum arrows it to use a metal detector, but not many bow hunters pack these gadgets. I try to use bright colored fletching, which helps a great deal. Make every effort to locate your arrow, or blood, as long as there is any doubt in your mind.

CHAPTER 6

THE WAITING GAME

*H*ow long to wait before taking up the trail of a wounded whitetail is a familiar question that has burdened deer hunters for years. This question is not only common, but important as well.

There has been reason to believe that to pursue the wounded whitetail too quickly could result in never recovering the animal. There has also been reason to believe that waiting to trail may result in the animal becoming stronger as time passes, making it more difficult to ever locate the quarry. We must look very carefully at reasons for and against waiting. How you play the waiting game after you have wounded a whitetail may very well determine whether or not you will ever recover it.

Many old timers claimed that after it had been wounded, the deer needed time to stiffen up. They felt it would find a place to bed down and, if not disturbed, would stiffen up while motionless and sick. If a hunter chased after too quickly, the animal would keep moving and never have a chance to stiffen.

I once believed that philosophy. Where ever you went, any state you hunted in, everybody thought a whitetail stiffened when wounded.

One old fellow I ran into gave me a handful of advice. I told him I hit a whitetail that morning, but since I had been unsure of my hit, decided to lay off trailing until mid afternoon, giving the arrow a chance to work. The guy told me the deer would stiffen in four to six hours in warm weather, two to three in cold weather. Since the temperature was in the 50's, he said the deer should be quite stiff and I could probably sneak up and dispose of it with another arrow, if needed.

Since this was 20 years ago, and I had only deer hunted for a few years, I was somewhat naive. I wasted no time going back, picked up the blood trail, found the deer dead, and another arrow not needed. Upon close inspection I found it was slightly stiff. Was this caused directly from death, or was the whitetail stiff before it perished?

The facts are that the stiffening up process does indeed occur, but it doesn't happen until death.

In a study conducted in the 1960's, John D. Gill, Maine Department of Inland Fisheries, and David C. O'Meara, Department of Animal Pathology, observed for a period of 2–13 days the carcasses of 85 deer shot by legal hunters and poachers. Reference data was done on temperature, eye appearance, pupil diameter, and rigor mortis patterns—or stiffening.

"Estimating Time Of Death In Whitetail Deer" was an article that appeared in the Journal Of Wildlife Management, Volume 29, No. 3, July, 1965. John Gill and David O'Meara were able to come up with many interesting and educating findings, and the article follows:

Figure 9   (see page 65)

Numbers of observations of rigor mortis in deer. (Journal of Wildlife Management, July 1965, John D. Gill and David C. O'Meara).

Rigor Mortis

Hours since Death

Rigor Mortis		1	2	3	4	5	6	7	8	9	10	11	12	13–18	19–24
Jaw	None	0													
	Partial	6	6												
	Stiff	1	18	28	24										
Neck	None	4	14	6	1										
	Partial	1	2	16	28	14	20	5	8	10	6	1	14		
	Stiff			1										25	13
Wrist (Carpus)	None	7	23	15	8	2	2								
	Partial	5	24	37	33	36	11	8	8	1					
	Stiff			1	5	4	15	11	16	21	15	11	25	45	25
Elbow*	None	7	10	20	12	10	5	3	3	4					
	Partial		12	20	38	29	49	12	28	22	20	12	26	51	32
	Stiff														
Ankle (Tarsus)	None	4	3	1	1			1	1						
	Partial	1	12	14	11	8	3	1	1	1	5	3	5	11	
	Stiff		2	12	16	16	18	7	6	7	3	3	5	5	
Knee†	None	4	2												
	Partial	1	12	5	3	1	2	1							
	Stiff		3	20	21	18	20	5	6					10	6

* The humerus, radius–ulna joint.
† The femur, tibia joint.

Rigor mortis was checked by gently attempting to flex various joints. This was done by grasping the outer end of the jaw (mandible), the upper end of the neck, the forelimb above and below either the wrist (corpus), or the elbow (humerus, radius–ulna joint), the hind leg above and below either the ankle (tarsus), or the knee (femur, fibular joint). Light pressure was exerted in the normal plane of movement of each part, except that necks were flexed up and down, not sideways. Care was taken not to reduce or break rigor, and the degree of stiffness present was recorded as "None", "1/4 inch", "1/2 inch", "3/4 inch", or "complete". Complete jaw, elbow, or knee rigor was quite firm, but the stage of wrist, ankle, and neck rigor which we considered complete was not entirely stiff. Stiffened wrist and ankle joints usually flexed enough to move the hoofs through an inch or two of arc, and complete neck rigor allowed even more movement.

Muscles gradually begin to stiffen soon after death, but later relax because of internal chemical changes. Rates of change depend on temperature and other factors, and differences in these factors produce different rates of stiffening in various parts of the body. In deer, we found the following sequence of stiffening more often than any other: jaw (first), knee, elbow, ankle, neck, and wrist (last). Exceptions were common, however, and were mostly due to the following four causes:

1. Wounds may prevent weaker or delay rigor in parts of the body near the tissue damage.

2. Rough handling of the carcass may either reduce or eliminate stiffening, depending on when the handling occurs.

3. Differences due to air temperature were not obvious in our data, but may have been masked by other variables.

4. Freezing results in stiffening which could be confused with rigor mortis. In air temperatures near 10°–15° F, the wrists of some deer froze within 4–6 hours after death.

The observations can be summarized as the hourly intervals when complete rigor was first present in a majority of the specimens. For example, jaws of 18 out of 24 deer were completely stiff at 2 hours (between 11/2 and 21/2 hours) post-mortem. Comparable intervals for the other parts were knee, 3 hours; elbow and ankle, 4; neck, 7; and wrist, 8 hours. The number of observations involved in this summary is given in Illustration 9 which shows the variation among all deer checked.

Sample numbers in Illustration 9 are low in relation to the total collection of 85 deer. This is partly due to the exclusions noted in Illustration 9, but also to the fact that other work prevented checking for rigor mortis on a regular schedule. Accordingly, comparisons in the illustration should only be made among the three rigor mortis stages of one part of a deer at a given time.

As previously noted jaws stiffened within 2 hours. Characteristically the lower jaw clamped tightly with the lips concealing the teeth although the tongue protruded. When the jaw started to relax, the front teeth became visible and the outer end of the jaw would flex about 1/4 inch. We did not observe such natural relaxation of the jaw in any deer dead less than 48 hours. Among 35 deer checked for jaw rigor after 2 days, two showed partial relaxation at 50 and 54 hours, but one was stiff 7 days after death. Among 15 deer which such relaxation was noted, it occurred during the third or fourth day in at least 8 and perhaps 10. In summary, jaw relaxation may indicate that the deer had been dead at least 2 days, probably for 3 or 4 days, but possibly for longer than 7 days,

The Journal Of Wildlife Management article concluded.

With these experiments conducted by John Gill and David O'Meara, we have basically determined that stiffening does not occur until after death. Their experiments can also help roughly determine how long a whitetail has been dead, after you have recovered it.

Now we know there is no reason to wait because of stiffening, before trailing a wounded whitetail. This myth should be pushed by the wayside. Is this reason alone a factor that should entice us to pursue a wounded whitetail more promptly? I say no. However, many experts feel there is still another reason to prompt us into immediate pursuit of a wounded whitetail, such as Professor Aaron N. Moen, Department Of Natural Resources, Cornell University, who in a 1970's study, determined the heart rates per minute for different activities through the year.

In the Journal of Wildlife Management, October, 1978, Professor Moen's report declared that:

- High r^2 values indicated that the annual pattern did indeed fit a sine wave.

- The highest r^2 values (all above 0.80) are for the 3 activities with the least movement; less variability in heart rates was observed when a deer was bedded, standing, or foraging than when walking. The r^2 for the running equation was 0.51; variations may be associated with fright responses. Visual and sound stimuli often caused an increase in heart rate that may be superimposed on the physical effect of running.

- A constant phase correction of 226 applies for heart rates during each of the 5 activities.

- Heart rates rank in order of increasing body movement.

The running whitetail has about three times the heart rate per minute of a bedded deer. Since the heart rate is increased on a moving whitetail, it is obvious that a wounded deer will bleed out considerably faster when pushed, than one that remains bedded.

Professor Moen, told me that, "We know from first aid that it is best to keep quiet when bleeding to reduce loss. A wounded deer may well bleed out faster when pushed and kept moving, but it will also be farther away."

In my opinion, Professor Moen couldn't have been more correct. Some experts believe that since the faster heart rate increases bleeding, this is reason to begin trailing immediately. They think that in cases of poor hits, the only chance to recover the animal is to bleed it out more quickly, either by external or internal bleeding. They feel that if a deer is left bedded it may bleed only a small amount, and a resting deer's wound will begin to coagulate with no further blood loss.

Other hunters believe the opposite, and I am in that group. I am convinced a moving deer will bleed out quicker, but I am not convinced that a wounded whitetail will always recover if left alone to rest. We must remember Professor Moen's comment, "But it will also be farther away." What good is a deer that is a half mile away, compared to one only 200 to 300 yards away? The farther you have to trail a whitetail, the less chance you have of recovering it.

I am a firm believer that any whitetail shot through the body cavity, either by gun or bow, will die eventually in most cases. Even though a whitetail is bedded, it continues to bleed internally, if shot through the body cavity.

Think of the paunch shot deer. When a whitetail has been gut shot, many times the intestines or stomach matter clogs the holes. Any deer hunter who has trailed paunch shot whitetails knows the blood trail is a slim one, sometimes no blood at all. Even though a moving deer is bleeding at a faster rate, the blood still does not get to the ground in many situations.

If we assume a paunch shot whitetail might live for four to six hours, if not pushed it will almost always bed down not far from where it was shot. If this is the case, we only have a short distance to trail in order to recover. On the other hand, if we push the whitetail to induce bleeding, we are certain to get it out of the first bed. It will probably run, bleeding out at a faster pace, but if it only lives for 30 more minutes, think of how much ground a deer might cover walking, much less running.

I have waited a few hours before taking up a trail on paunch shot whitetails, but still found them alive in their beds. If I am not able to dispose of the animal, usually it will get up, walk only a short distance and bed down again. Therefore, when I jump the animal I let it go again, if weather permits, and return an hour or so later to begin trailing. By then the deer is usually dead.

My assumption is that anyone who pushes a paunch shot whitetail is very unlikely to recover it. Beginners may make this mistake, but experienced hunters are well aware of the consequences. Hunters who think a deer will bleed out quicker when pushed, and decide to trail immediately, make a grave mistake.

Experience has taught me that the paunch shot deer does not want to move. It is hurt and knows it must rest for its own benefit, keeping to a minimum the distance between the point at which shot to the point where it beds.

Many years back I bow shot a small buck about 7:30 a.m. The shot was only 15 yards, but obstructions did not allow me to see exactly where the arrow hit. Close inspection convinced me that I had probably gut shot the buck.

I left the area quietly and decided to allow time for the arrow to do its job. I returned at 10 with a couple of hunters and would have waited longer, but rain was forecast and I couldn't risk it. We trailed the buck for about 200 yards when one of the hunters spotted it walking slowly away with head down. We had jumped the buck, so decided to leave and give it a couple more hours. The blood trail had been difficult to follow, and we knew if we pushed the buck we were likely to lose it.

We returned about 1 p.m., found the bed that it had spent the morning in, searched frantically for a trail, but came up with nothing. It was apparent no blood was getting to the ground. Since we had seen which direction the buck had taken, we concentrated in that area. After 30 minutes I finally spotted the buck under a large, shady oak tree. I eased up in case another shot would be needed, but the buck was already in the promised land.

I had been fortunate to know the direction the buck had taken. If my companions had not seen the deer, there was a good chance we might never have recovered this deer. If this buck had been pushed, I am certain it would have been a hopeless situation. This buck was recovered simply because of well planned trailing.

The old standby rule of thumb has usually been to wait at least 30 minutes before taking up the trail after a lung or heart shot. I see no reason to wait this long, provided you are positive about your hit, since the animal is doomed to a quick death.

The bow hunter sometimes sees the arrow make a good hit. Whenever I am in this situation, I sometimes take up trailing immediately, or after a 15 minute wait. If I am uncertain, only thinking there is a chance I hit the vitals, I will wait longer before taking up the trail. There is nothing to lose by waiting a short while. A whitetail hit in the heart or lungs will surely die. It will go only a short distance in the time you wait to begin trailing.

The gun hunter usually does not know for sure that he hit a vital spot, but can be almost certain if the shot was taken at an apparently easy mark at close yardage, and is relatively sure he was on target. If he takes up the trail immediately, he may be able to determine if the shot was in the vitals. If he leaves the whitetail alone, usually no harm is done, then begins trailing again when it is time. If the gun hunter assumes he has made a good hit, it is not necessary to wait as the whitetail will be only a short distance ahead.

The liver hit, the same as the paunch shot, either by broadhead or bullet, will kill but not quickly. The liver hit causes internal bleeding and eventual death. However, the hunter has to give the animal time to succumb.

The liver hit whitetail, if pushed, will bleed out faster, since the heart rate increases. But, just as the paunch shot, can be difficult to trail.

As a rule the liver hit deer will leave a slightly better blood trail than the paunch shot deer, but the entry or departure hole can become clogged with tissue or stomach matter to make it nearly impossible to trail by blood alone.

Even though the liver shot whitetail dies slowly, it perishes sooner than the paunch shot deer. I have found from experience that the liver hit deer should be given two hours. It will usually bed down quickly after being hit and be close to that original bed when found.

On two occasions I found that two hours' waiting was not enough on a liver hit deer. Both times I backed up and left the deer alone for another hour, then recovered near the location where they were last seen. As with the paunch shot deer, both bedded down again when left alone, making recovery easier.

The kidney shot deer dies quickly from hemorrhage, requiring no waiting time before trailing. The real problem is knowing for a fact that you hit the kidneys. Since they are very small, it is luck when they are punctured by a bullet or a broadhead.

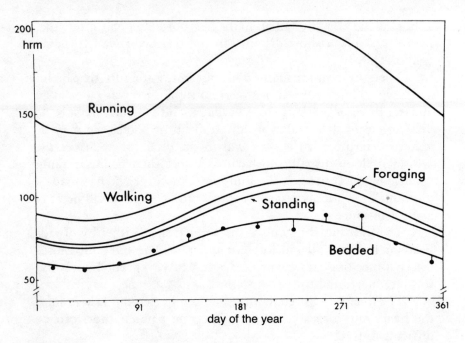

Figure 10
Predicted heart rates per minute during 5 different activities throughout the year. (Aaron N. Moen, Journal Of Wildlife Management, October, 1978).

I believe most kidney hits must be regarded as a gut shot deer as it is usual to puncture intestines also. The kidney hit will bleed well, even externally, one way of knowing there is a chance you hit the kidneys after a gut shot. Blood color, another factor in determining a kidney hit, will be discussed in another chapter.

Whitetails spine shot, or hit near the spine, will sometimes manage to crawl off. This is a deer you should go after immediately, simply because there will be a chance you can finish it off. Trailing immediately not only increases your chance of recovery, but is the humane thing to do, since many have to be shot again in these circumstances.

Others to be trailed immediately are the artery and the meat hits as the induced heart rate will lead you to this deer. The major arteries, when severed, will bleed a deer out very rapidly and it will be recovered in a short distance.

Meat hits, such as neck, rump, or loin area, have smaller blood vessels that can still kill if the right tactics are used. I firmly believe a deer hit in these areas should be trailed at once. The hunter should consistently push the animal to increase the heart rate and cause faster bleeding. Since bleeding is the only way you can ever recover this deer, keep it moving. I think it's best to trail slowly and quietly so you will not have it running hard and fast, and trailing is not as difficult.

Meat hits can easily be determined by the bow hunters, usually because he can see where the arrow hits, and the gun hunter can sometimes tell by the deer's reaction. The blood trail is usually good on a meat hit, especially during the first 200 yards.

Many deer hunters choose to trail all wounded deer immediately, simply because they don't have the patience to wait. They seem to be in a hurry to slip that tag around an antler or leg and know they have become successful. There were times, particularly in my beginning deer hunting days, when I found it difficult to sit back and wait, but I have trained myself.

Many choose to wait before trailing any wounded whitetail, regardless of where the deer has been hit. It is important to know which hits warrant immediate trailing, in some cases the only chance to recover the animal. The hunter must remember these to ensure chances of success, and to eliminate the possibility a whitetail may perish and never be found.

It is important to remember how long to wait. Waiting one hour, when it should be four hours, could be as big a mistake as trailing immediately. On the other hand, trailing after waiting 30 minutes, when it should have been two hours, is just as poor judgment.

If a hunter puts himself in the situation of a wounded whitetail, he might see why the animal would choose to bed down close to where it was hit. It can't be much fun running or walking around with a hole in you. The whitetail feels discomfort and pain, requiring rest. This is not always the case, especially if the animal has gone into shock, but applies in most situations where death has been prolonged.

To keep from trailing too quickly we basically must prepare mentally. We know it is going to be much easier to recover a deer that has gone only 200 yards, compared to a half-mile or more. We know there is a better chance of success by having to trail a whitetail only a short distance.

In summary, this chapter has taught many things. In reality a deer does not stiffen up before death, so there is no need to hesitate trailing because of this. We learned that to push a wounded whitetail increases the deer's heart rate, which in turn speeds up blood loss, but puts a deer farther away causing the more difficult trailing.

We learned which types of body hits require immediate trailing and which require the hunter to wait a given amount of time, and how waiting or not waiting can hurt or help.

If a deer hunter remembers these things, he will certainly increase chances of success. Even though a hunter has scouted his quarry well, set up the perfect ambush location, made the shot to the best of his ability, he must play the waiting game correctly. The waiting game is an important factor after a hit. Take it just as seriously as the hunt itself.

CHAPTER 7

HOW WEATHER AND DARKNESS AFFECT TRAILING

Weather and darkness are important factors in a decision on whether or not to begin trailing. Even though you may or may not consider the hit a vital one, weather conditions may prompt your trailing, or darkness may delay trailing.

With a morning hit, there is no darkness to be concerned with. Even if it might be a paunch shot, requiring several hours of waiting, you will be able to trail before dark. Since deer hunting is done frequently in the evening, particularly from ambush locations, a hunter many times shoots at dusk, or just before. Then comes that important question of trailing or waiting.

The first concern is where the deer has been hit. If waiting is implied, then by all means wait until morning to trail, if weather permits. Many times the hunter may have to work the next morning. Others sometimes think that, since they are there, they should go ahead and trail.

To me, work is the only reason to cause a hunter to trail before morning, but even so you may be able to trail for a couple of hours before work. If there is no way to wait until morning, leave quietly and go home. You can return in a few hours with the proper lighting and extra help, even if it means coming back at midnight. It is better than pushing the animal too early in the dark.

If I am unsure of my hit just before dark, many times the case in poor lighting, I will usually attempt to trail the deer that night, at least far enough to determine what kind of a hit I made. Sometimes it may only be 50 yards or less to determine by blood color alone the kind of hit.

A bow hunter has an advantage, if fortunate enough to recover the arrow, to read its signs. The other way is to watch the animal closely when you shoot. The deer's reaction and how it leaves the scene will assist you in knowing whether or not you hit. Many hunters, including myself, have been in a tree at dark wondering if a hit was made.

The meat hit that requires pushing the animal is immediately a problem at dusk. It is next to impossible to trail a whitetail in darkness and hope for a second shot. It is dangerous, illegal in some areas, and many states don't allow you in the woods with a weapon after dark. The wise choice is to trail the animal slowly for a couple of hours and hope the whitetail might go down. If not successful in recovering this deer, return home and wait for morning, then hope for the best the next day.

If the hunter is fairly certain of a good hit, the deer should be trailed at once. Why risk weather conditions or other factors that may mess up your schedule the following morning. A deer hit through the vitals will be close by. The blood trail should be easy to follow, even in total darkness.

I would gladly trade for daytime trailing anytime. Everything shows up better, it is easier to see blood, and far easier to spot a dead deer.

I have been on more than one night trailing job when the deer was not found, even though it was within a few feet of where I walked. The deer is easily recovered the next morning, simply because visibility is so much better.

When you trail a deer at night, use proper lighting. Many think battery operated lights work well, just because they have a big light, but this isn't so. The best type is a gas powered lantern, far better illumination and you are sure to spot blood easier.

I have found it best to trail at night with one or two other persons. Not only do you feel safer from the "boogie-man", but you can use one person as a marker. When trailing during the daytime you can rely on markers, but in the dark it is next to impossible to see them from a short distance. With another hunter as a marker, holler now and then and keep yourself going in a given direction. I have used my wife on occasion, if none of my hunting buddies were available. I put her on the last blood marker and when I find more blood, she moves forward to the new spot. We continue this until we recover the deer, or until we have lost the trail without hope. The only thing I have against this system is noise, but I think the pros far surpass the cons.

Another concern with night trailing is getting lost. An area you know well in the daytime may be completely strange in the dark. I think I know quite well some areas I hunt year after year, but in the dark I find myself mixed up, guessing which direction to go next.

I remember one night trailing job I helped on, along with my son and two others. My son hit a deer just before dark and it was about as black as the ace of spades when we began trailing. We lost the trail in a couple hundred yards and gave up until morning. We started back, discussing the hit deer, and finally one guy asked if anybody knew the way out. I pointed in a particular direction and we began walking, but it wasn't long before everyone realized I didn't know what I was talking about. Fortunately, one of the others picked a direction that soon led us out, only a short distance from our vehicles.

Even though you think you know an area well, never take it for granted in the dark. You will swear the terrain changed while you were there. Although you can locate your blind in the dark, using a flashlight, you have usually established a direct path. Once you get off it, you can easily end up lost.

Take notice of the area before you begin trailing at night. If there is a nearby road or highway, you may hear traffic during the quiet night hours. Known fences may also help if you become lost. Sometimes, in an unfamiliar area, locate a topographic map of that quadrangle. I own about 30 topo maps, and they have helped more than once. You can locate drainages, creeks, open areas, many things to help when trailing. Even though these are not easily seen in the dark, they can help when you come across one.

One poor fellow trailed a deer alone one night, became aware that he was lost, but that area of southern Indiana didn't put him in any immediate danger. If you walk one straight direction for a short period in this part of the state, you are certain to bump into a road. However, he had trouble walking straight in an old strip mine area that covered about two square miles. After about three hours of hopeless walking, he remembered there was an extremely tall radio tower with a red light on top, not far from where he had started trailing. He climbed a tree, spotted the tower, and wasted no time in getting out.

I have spent a lot of nights eating burnt suppers through the deer hunting months. My wife knows it is not uncommon for me to arrive late now and then, especially since I do a lot of hunting in the evening, and if I am not home 30 minutes or so after dark, someone has hit a deer. On some occasions I am home soon after, but other times as late as midnight. I am sure many readers have operated under these circumstances.

I will always pick day over night trailing, if there is a choice, but many times I have to trail when necessary. Using the correct procedures can be rewarding and enjoyable.

A hunter should be aware of weather predictions before he decides to put off trailing until morning. Rain or snow in the forecast will change the whole situation. If I feel I have gut or liver shot a whitetail, and the forecast calls for a 50 percent or better chance of rain or snow, I will take my chance and trail the deer within the next couple of hours. If the forecast is less than that, I might decide to risk it and wait until morning.

I live in the southern part of Indiana, and snow is seldom seen until January or later, and is rare during the deer season. When we get snow at this time, it is generally light and doesn't create much of a problem. My main concern is rain, which comes frequently in the fall.

Hunters in northern regions will usually see snow, particularly in the latter part of the season. They are aware that snow will erase a blood trail, just as rain will do.

Some years back, on the night before Thanksgiving, my dad knocked a buck down just before dark, but was unsure of his hit. Since rain was in the forecast, we had no choice but to take up the trail shortly after dark. We found blood easily the first 100 yards and had hopes of recovering the buck anytime. A light rain started to fall, and within 10 minutes the diluted blood was difficult to see, and after another 10 minutes all traces were gone. We spent another hour searching, but never could locate the buck. We came back the next morning but were finally forced to give it up.

Anyone who has trailed whitetails in the rain should be aware of how fast a blood trail can be wiped out. Even though the rain might be light, it eventually soaks everything and watered down blood is no longer that crimson red. Sometimes the only way to tell is to wipe it with your fingers to see if it smears a little color.

Many who hunt during the rain have to be ready for the consequences. If you shoot, take only shots you are confident about. This should be the case regardless of weather, but is even more important during a rain. A good lung and heart shot deer will go down soon enough, but poor hits are liable to end up with the deer wasting away.

Even though rain or snow may have eliminated the blood trail, it is no reason to abandon a search. You still should spend a considerable amount of time on the chance you might locate the deer. It might be best to have several other hunters assist, a situation where the more eyes you have looking, the better chance of someone spotting the deer.

Some areas provide tracks to assist you, even though they may not appear fresh because of the rain. When rain falls, everything becomes saturated. The ground is softer and your deer may leave tracks. If the deer is in a heavily wooded area, leaves will curl and push down further as the deer steps on them. Dry

Photo by Leonard Lee Rue III.

leaves do not push. If you are not too far behind the deer, this sign will be obvious enough to follow by tracks alone, if you trail patiently and don't hurry.

If a light snow begins falling when you are trailing a deer, don't panic as your trail will be not covered that quickly. If the snow melts as it hits the ground, it will water down the blood, as does rain. However, the slower process will give you more time to recover a deer. I would rather trail a deer in light snow than in light rain. Heavy snow, sticking to the ground, will wipe out a trail quickly, but right behind the deer, you may be able to follow by tracks alone. Heavy snow will cover blood quickly, but allows more time to locate the deer before all tracks are eliminated. If you are able to get close to the deer, you can follow its tracks through the snow, making it easier.

Cold weather has a great effect as blood on the ground for only a couple of minutes will freeze if the temperatures are in the low 20's or less. When blood freezes, it becomes more difficult to see, and this is no time to judge a hit by the color, as after it freezes blood becomes darker. Even bright colored blood from a good lung hit will appear darker, resembling that of a liver hit.

Frost is also a major problem. Many times I have shot whitetails in the evening and let them go until morning. Although temperatures might only be in the 30's, if it is a clear night frost may arrive. I have seen blood trails, excellent the night before, become difficult to see by morning because of frost. When you are following blood under normal conditions it is fairly easy to see because of its luster and the brilliance really seems to stand out. After a frost it is very blunt, almost colorless. Trail much slower or you will lose it.

Blood in the open tends to burn when in sunshine for a long period. It dries out faster and becomes duller which, like frost covered blood, is harder to see. However, I would rather follow a blood trail exposed to the sun than one that has been covered by frost. It does not seem to burn as much.

Unfavorable weather not only makes hunting miserable, but also can cost you a deer. Rain in particular creates a great problem for anyone involved in trailing whitetails. Many hunters can blame this culprit every year for an unfilled tag. It has cost me a few deer and will probably cost me a few more, but we just make most of this situation. Even though a blood trail is lost, do not abandon a search. Every possible effort should be put into attempting to recover the deer. You will feel better and the whitetail you shot certainly deserves it.

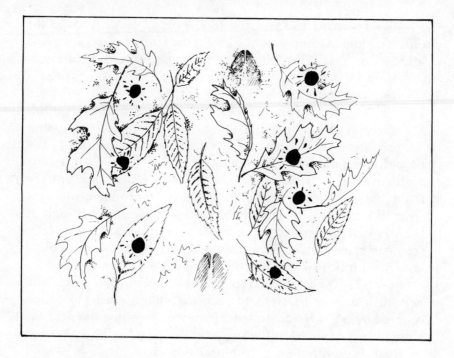

Figure 11
If the shot has completely penetrated the deer, two trails may be found.
Illustration by Larry Smail.

CHAPTER 8

THE ART OF TRAILING

I sincerely believe that trailing is a true art, a function that many hunters do quite easily, but others find difficult. However, anyone who practices, or is taught by experienced hunters, will eventually learn to trail skillfully. I have seen beginners jump right in and trail a wounded whitetail as though they had done it all their lives. On the other hand, others who have hunted for several years still seem to lack enough knowledge to trail a whitetail alone.

My first experience came in my first year of deer hunting, after another hunter had shot a small buck. I remember it well, mainly because I enjoyed it so much. I took a great interest in the correct procedures, how exciting it was to round the next bend, not knowing what to expect. It was a very happy moment when a fellow hunter hollered "There it is!" Although it wasn't my deer, I still felt the excitement of the kill.

I am still excited some 25 years later and enthusiastic when I participate in trailing a wounded whitetail. It seems as though I learn something new each year, and certainly don't consider I know it all, or that anyone knows all about trailing. Some days

I seem able to trail more effectively, other days everything goes right or goes wrong. If it is a bad day, one of my companions will usually pick up the trail and take over. I have great faith in a few of my hunting partners' abilities.

This chapter is to help you become a better trailer, to know what to look for. I will not go into detail on how to trail hits that pertain to particular parts of the body. This will be done in the following four chapters, since hit locations drastically change trailing techniques. This chapter will outline the basic fundamentals of following a blood trail, as well as trailing without blood. Even an experienced trailer may pick up a few pointers, as I did while doing research on this book. The beginning hunter should gain a considerable amount of knowledge and a more positive, confident attitude towards trailing.

Assume that you have already marked the spot where your whitetail left, and waited a reliable amount of time. One of the first questions is, should I seek help, or should I trail alone? If time and weather permit, I have found it best to trail with one or two others, that any more will only hinder your procedures. Take into consideration how much more noise is involved, which could push your deer much farther ahead. With too many people walking around, there is a good chance blood may be stomped out before it is seen. Usually, as a blood trail is lost, everyone fans out and starts looking, and a meager trail no longer exists.

When I have two people help me it is nice to use one for a "last blood marker", the other to help look for blood as four eyes do a better job than two. You can whistle to the standing person to move ahead whenever new blood is found. This creates no major disturbance.

Be sure and stay to the outside edges of your blood trail, then blood on leaves is not rolled over if you are forced to backtrack.

When you must trail alone, mark your trail as you go to keep yourself on line and know which direction the whitetail is going. By marking your line you keep yourself from accidentally backtracking, which is easier than you think in unfamiliar territory or in the dark. I always carry an abundant amount of toilet paper, and a small piece tied in a bowtie fashion marks a spot well. In extremely thick cover I tie these every 10 yards or so, because if too far apart they can become lost from vision. In more open woods I tie them every 30 to 40 yards, about head high, to enable you to see them more easily when you look back. When I trail a deer that is leaving blood signs several yards apart, I usually tie at each spot. The nice thing about toilet paper is that it decomposes after a couple of good rain showers.

I have found it easier to trail someone else's deer than one I have wounded, simply because I am not as excited or nervous. The person who shot is more emotional, probably human nature, so an assistant is an advantage.

One significant factor is patience, preached to us by experts to make us better hunters, and also extremely important when trailing. Anyone overanxious is more apt to miss good sign, or even lose a trail, sooner than someone who is calm and patient, so this is where the extra person will help. A person who has shot a deer is always looking ahead, trying to spot the downed deer, and when in a hurry reduces chances of recovery.

Blood is seldom found at the location the deer was hit, in fact, it may be 10 to 20 yards or more away. It is rare if blood is found immediately.

The hit location will determine how soon blood may be found. What the arrow or bullet hits as it passes through the deer, and how high the entry and departure hole, bears on how soon the animal begins bleeding. An arrow that exits through the bottom of the chest cavity, as compared to an arrow six inches higher, will cause dropping blood much quicker. If the shot was on a walking or running whitetail, the blood will not accelerate as promptly, especially if the front leg is back when a hit was made. As the whitetail departs, the leg is shifted back and forth, sometimes blocking the hole and not allowing blood to get to the ground. On other moving hits, hide shifting will produce the same result.

Some hits produce a better blood trail as time goes on, so the farther you trail the more amplified it becomes. With a low departing hole the body cavity continues filling with blood, which leaks out more frequently. On a high departing hole this is just the opposite as the body cavity never fills up to the point of the exit. As the whitetail continues bleeding inside, less blood gets to the ground and this trail becomes more difficult to follow.

Many hits, such as the paunch shot, may clog the holes so less blood will drip, even though you have a low exit hole and the body cavity continues to fill up from internal bleeding. Many times I have heard hunters make the statement, "This deer isn't hurt bad," just because little or no blood is found. In all reality, this deer may be hurt far worse than one bleeding a great deal, but trailing is more difficult, which can lessen your chances of recovery because the trail is more adverse, not because the whitetail is not hurt.

A great deal of blood being found might represent an artery hit and a quick recovery. Other times meat hits will bleed profusely at first, causing you to think the deer will go down soon, but bleeding will generally slow up after a couple of hundred yards and leave you scratching your head. The lung, liver and heart shots all bleed differently and will be discussed in following chapters.

The main thing is not to take for granted, because a blood trail is slim, that the deer can't be found. This has no bearing on how badly the deer is hurt. Trailing must be done more patiently, with more time and effort applied, but this deer can be recovered.

Blood can tell a lot. It may tell by color alone where the deer was hit and if a deer is running or standing. By learning all these factors you will become a better trailer and boost your chances of recovery.

One way of telling if an arrow or bullet has penetrated the deer completely is by taking notice of the blood trail. If doubled, appearing like two trails instead of one, complete penetration has been made. Usually both trails will be a little to the outside of the tracks, if they are visible.

Sometimes, even though you made complete penetration, only one trail may exist because one hole is higher. Look closely

Figure 12
A deer walking slowly or standing in one spot will leave blood drops in round
shapes with splatter marks surrounding the drops completely.
Illustration by Larry Smail.

and you may still find an occasional drop spaced apart from the
main blood trail, which is usually about one to one and one-half
feet apart.

There are times when a double blood trail may not represent complete penetration. Not long after I began bow hunting,
a fellow hunter shot a small buck, saw a great deal of his arrow

Figure 13
A running deer will leave irregular teardrop shaped blood spots, with splatter marks at the top of the drops, which indicate which direction the deer is going.
Illustration by Larry Smail.

sticking out of the deer, and assumed he hit the shoulder blade with minimal penetration. We trailed a single line blood trail for about 200 yards, then hit a double trail, which we followed for about 30 yards when it finally ended. We searched frantically for more blood, but never came up with anything. Upon close inspection of the double blood trail we found a track, the hoof print leading back toward the direction the deer was shot. We realized the buck had doubled back, causing the other blood trail a short distance from the first. We backtracked to where the deer veered off, trailed it for a short period and lost the trail, satisfied the hit was not lethal.

Blood drops can tell you if the whitetail is running or walking. A standing deer will leave blood that appears more clustered, instead of going in a direct line. The direction a deer is traveling is indicated by splatter marks, always at the top of the blood spot to show the forward direction of the deer. If you lose a blood trail and pick it up again a distance away, this can show you the course a deer is taking and save accidental backtracking.

The type of country and terrain, or types of soil, may determine how easy it is to find blood. While hunting in Colorado for mule deer and elk, I have noticed blood seems to soak into the ground and is almost impossible to see. Since there are not many leaves on the ground, this can cause difficult trailing. In Indiana, blood can be seen on bare dirt, but I still prefer a cover of leaves or other debris to catch the blood. Anything shows blood better than bare dirt.

I have trailed whitetails through almost any kind of terrain you can imagine, but harvested cornfields show up blood better than anything else, excluding snow. When the field is picked, the husks and remains pretty well cover the ground, leaving very little bare dirt. Almost every drop of blood hits something you can easily see. Since corn is a light tan, blood shows up extremely well, so trying to determine the type of hit you have from blood color alone is more easily done in a cornfield than any other place, providing the animal is shot standing in the field. Your chances otherwise are slim.

When a whitetail you are trailing cuts across an open cornfield, this is helpful as you will locate blood more easily. One disappointment, however, is that you can probably see completely across the field and tell if your deer is not yet down. If the field is 200 to 300 yards across, you know it has gone at least that far, so hopes for an early recovery are gone.

I believe it unlikely for a mortally wounded deer to cross a wide open field intentionally. In most cases a deer hit through the body cavity will look for thick cover in which to bed down. I have trailed whitetails that were hit in a leg or hip across open fields. These just want to put distance between you, especially if it knows you are following close behind.

I am grateful to be able to trail a wounded whitetail through woods instead of thickets. When leaves completely cover the woods floor, most of the blood drops on top of the leaves, enabling you to find it. Some leaves cause a problem because of color, turning in the fall to a reddish cast to almost match blood color. This is especially true with maple, some leaves completely red and others red-spotted. Many times a hunter will holler that he has found blood, but upon close examination discovers it is only a red spot on the leaf. One way to tell is to wet your fingers and wipe the spot. Even dried blood will wipe off. If you take for granted it is blood, without wetting it, you may throw yourself off and won't find the correct trail.

Since I do a great deal of hunting in thick cover, I am forced to trail whitetails in unpreferred areas, which I don't like but have no choice. Very few leaves exist in these areas so there is no floor to show blood. Many times I have trailed a whitetail easily through woods, but lost it in the thickets. Even though the whitetail may still be bleeding, you swear the blood has just stopped.

If you are fortunate enough to have a deer cross a honeysuckle patch, you might find blood again. Honeysuckles cover things very well and provide a base for blood to catch on, just like cornfields or woods. Since the honeysuckle is dark green, blood shows up quite readily.

When trailing through thick cover expect to be slowed up but not halted, but a little more patience and effort on your part is needed to continue. Try not to get too far ahead of yourself when the blood trail is lost, as many tend to do in hopes of picking up new blood.

I have trailed a wounded whitetail through fairly open woods, have it turn into thickets and I became excited. This is what a severely wounded whitetail will do in many cases, turn to the thick cover to bed down and you may recover it soon. A doe I once trailed through about 300 yards of open woods

Figure 14
Check rocks and trees as well as high grass for blood smears.
Illustration by Larry Smail.

finally made an abrupt right turn into a thick honeysuckle
patch. I found it dead, lying in bed with its head tucked between
the front hooves. This deer used the thick cover for security,
as many whitetails will do, more comfortable than lying out
in an open woods. I feel certain it was able to stay concealed in
the thickets and still be able to overlook the backtrail through
the woods.

Broom sage, or high grass fields, weeds that may reach
three feet or more off the ground, also present a problem for the
trailer. Blood will wipe off the side of the deer onto the broom
sage, not onto the ground, but you may see the sage knocked
down or leaning away, all you need to get you back on trail.
Check the grass to see if blood has smeared on it. If the deer had

been bleeding well, blood is certain to wipe off although it is difficult to see. I hate to see a whitetail turn into a fairly open sage field, but it provides good cover, just as thickets do.

Don't be heartbroken when the deer suddenly decides to cross a road as this does not mean it is not hurt. I have had whitetails cross several roads before succumbing, but another hunter driving along may spot the deer.

A small buck I had paunch shot and jumped once decided to cross a road, so I decided to abandon trailing for the time being. Just then a vehicle stopped where the deer had crossed and a hunter hollered that he had seen a deer in the thickets. Two men grabbed their weapons and began pursuit. I hollered at them to leave it alone, let them know the whitetail was gut shot and that I planned to resume trailing later. Both agreed, although I worried that they would return while I waited. I was greatly relieved to find the buck about three hours later, only 100 yards from where it crossed the road.

Many whitetails when hit will follow a deer trail for several hundred yards. I think poorly hit whitetails are more apt to do this than deer hit through the vitals. Many may run the first 50 to 100 yards through extremely thick cover, but eventually end up on a designated trail, an easy access for one to find new blood.

Many beginning hunters expect to find a great deal of blood when trailing a wounded whitetail, but this is seldom the case. Sometimes only specks of blood may be visible, but even though you find only a small amount, each drop gets you a little closer to a possible recovery.

Many hunters fail to check hilltops or hillsides because they don't think a hurt whitetail will climb up. I might have believed this, mostly because of trailing in flatland regions, but after hunting in Kentucky hills I found things a little different. I have seen well hit whitetails go towards the top after being shot at the bottom of a hill. They generally go up by angling along the side, rather than going straight up. I think it has the intention of either bedding down on top, or going to a particular thicket or water hole.

It is rare for a wounded whitetail to run a straight line, providing it is not vitally hit and going down quickly. Almost all whitetails will circle. The farther the whitetail goes, the closer back the circle comes. I have trailed many for a mile or more that have ended up within 100 yards of where they were shot, I assume because it is a home territory.

About the only time whitetails have not circled back when trailed a long distance involved a buck during the rut. I have seen wounded bucks go at least 1 1/2 miles, almost as straight as a line, probably because they were out of their normal home range.

Patience is an important factor when trailing. Some blood trails could be followed on a dead run, but going slowly, quietly, is the best practice. Don't be afraid to get close to the ground as too much blood is missed by standing up. Bend over and get your eyes close to the ground, and in cases where blood is scarce, get on your hands and knees. I have lost a blood trail, tried desperately to pick it back up, but could not until I was on all four's. A couple of feet closer can make a difference. I have had to trail like this for a long distance, because only specks of blood were visible.

It pays to keep your ears open as you trail as well as your eyes. If you participate in enough trailing experiences, sooner or later you will approach close enough to a bedded whitetail so you will actually see it get out of bed or at least hear it depart. Seriously wounded whitetails will let a hunter get extremely close on occasion, especially if bedded in thick cover. I guess they feel they might not be seen, since whitetails do the same thing in good health.

A seriously hurt bedded whitetail will usually get out of bed in a slow fashion, and tend to sneak out rather than go at a fast pace. Sometimes the gun hunter has time to pick another shot as the whitetail leaves. Trailing quietly, you may get the opportunity.

Keep in mind that blood does not always land in ideal spots. Many trail effectively at a fast pace as long as they have leaves to spot blood on. As soon as the blood is lost, they often give up and decide the whitetail must have recovered. Many

Figure 15

(A) Trail of a deer shot through brisket with leg broken low in shoulder. (B) Trail of a deer shot high through the shoulders. (C) Trail of a deer with a broken foreleg—the lower the leg is broken, the more pronounced the drag mark. (D) Trail of a deer with a broken hind leg—the lower the leg is broken, the more pronounced the drag mark. (E) Trail of a deer shot through the ham. (F) This trail usually means that the animal was shot through the intestines, liver or lungs; the animal will not go much over a mile, even if not given time to get sick; death results in less than two hours. (G) Same as F but did not penetrate to the lungs. The animal dies slowly, and after a couple of hours is usually shot in its bed. (H) The cross jump results from a bullet through the intestines or liver with the animal standing broadside to the hunter—usually the slowest killing shot.

(Joseph Brunner, TRACKS AND TRACKING).

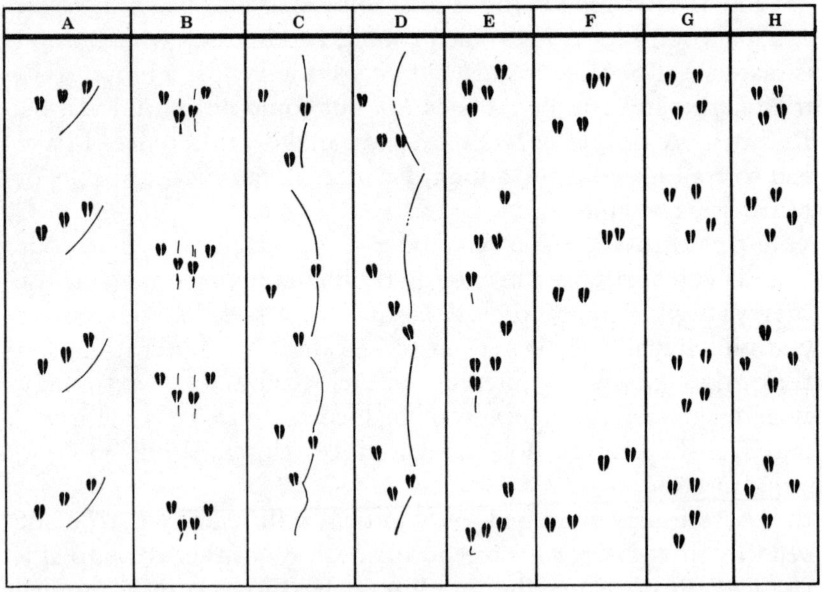

times it will pay, particularly in areas where a lot of the ground dirt is exposed, to pay close attention to trees and rocks, which will show blood as will high grass and branches. The blood, even though it has stopped dripping, will smear on anything the deer rubs against. If you have had a good blood trail for a long distance, the hide has become saturated and will wipe off on anything. Finding blood on trees or high grass can indicate how high the hit is.

I have trailed whitetails where the arrow has punched through the underneath belly of the deer. This will smear on top of bushes and high grass as a whitetail goes over the top, and this type of trail will usually last longer than the smeared blood trail. A low departure will bleed more freely as the whitetail moves and keeps wiping off. The sides of the deer's body will eventually be wiped reasonably clean and stop smearing. Check for smears when your blood trail has suddenly stopped as they can be found when all else fails.

When you have trailed a deer as far as you can, and have not recovered it, resort to trailing by tracks, or signs of disturbance where the deer has passed through.

Tall grass and weeds will be bent or knocked down, more so when the whitetail is running than walking. The walking whitetail will leave signs such as leaves turned over and rustled looking, or if the woods floor is damp, the hooves will push the leaves down and slightly curled. You may be fortunate enough to trail a deer through a woods if older prints don't mingle with your original trail.

The easiest trailing of all will be in snow. You have probably heard the old expression, "that guy couldn't track an elephant in four feet of snow", but I reckon anyone could handle that. But trailing in snow can be confusing at times, particularly when several other tracks merge. Be sure the tracks you are following are fresh.

Blood shows up easily on snow, red on white, as long as the whitetail continues bleeding. Hunters in northern areas, where snow is abundant during the season, have recovery chances in a higher bracket than the hunter who has to trail without snow.

The simplest way to trail a wounded whitetail when blood has stopped, or at least slacked off to a bare minimum, is by tracks alone. Tracks can tell a great deal. In 1909 a German, Joseph Brunner, registered eight different sets of tracks of wounded whitetails. Each represented a different type of wound.

I do not know if Mr. Brunner's recordings are correct, since I have never really studied the track patterns of a wounded whitetail, and I was not aware of these findings until I began research for this book. However, I am anxious to study these patterns in future trailing opportunities. I have noticed a different pattern when a whitetail has been hit through the ham or legs, and it is understandable since the deer's walking or running method has to be changed. I am even more curious to check the liver, intestinal, or lung shot patterns.

The front hooves are somewhat larger than the back hooves. The average walking adult whitetail track will average 2½ to 3 inches in length, larger in some deer. The running tracks of the adult whitetail will average 3½ to 4 inches wide, which includes the dew claws, visible on the running deer track. In softer terrain, snow or mud, dew claws are visible on the walking whitetail. The dew claws on the front are closer to the hoof than on the hind feet. The tracks of larger bucks are usually somewhat wider and longer than most doe tracks, and some measure up to 4½ inches, definitely a keeper.

The walking whitetail will leave tracks spaced about as far apart as an adult man walking. I have noticed this many times along the edges of fields or old dirt roads.

The tracks of fawns or six month old whitetails will be noticeable due to size, especially when the doe is with the young one. Usually the six month old, when shot, will not try to run off with the doe. The older doe, that has young with her, usually takes off in any direction away from the hit location. I have never been able to tell if a wounded young whitetail tries to get back to its mother. Sometimes when a hunter has shot a whitetail doe in the morning, another hunter returns in the evening and manages to take one of the younger whitetails.

The running whitetail brings its back feet ahead of the front, and this way is able to push off with more power. When the whitetail runs, its tracks will be in sets of fours, spaced around 2½ to 3 feet apart.

It is helpful to know if the deer you are trailing is walking or running. If you have been trailing for a reasonable distance, and the tracks suddenly change from a walking to a running

Figure 16
Common track pattern of a walking whitetail. Illustration by Larry Smail.

Figure 17
Common track pattern of a running whitetail. Illustration by Larry Smail.

pattern, it could very well be an indication the whitetail had either seen or heard you.

Many hunters declare that they can determine the sex of a whitetail by the tracks alone. I am not sure if there has been proof to back up the statements, but I can not tell under some circumstances. The buck track will appear heavier and larger as a rule, particularly on larger bucks, but some does outweigh some bucks, causing them to sink deeper on a soft surface.

Buck tracks can be distinguished from doe tracks after a snowfall. The buck will leave a slight drag mark, where the doe raises its feet up and walks in a more delicate fashion.

The hoof is designed to give the deer extremely good footing on hard surfaces. However, the hunter who pursues the whitetail across ice will probably catch up with his quarry. The deer has a difficult time trying to walk or run on ice, and after it slips and falls, it is unlikely to get to its feet again.

Whitetail hooves are very sharp and can cause great harm to an approaching human. It will use hooves for protection, so always approach a downed whitetail from the backside.

After the hunter has lost all blood sign and there are no tracks to follow, there is still another method which has worked well for me, called the loop.

At your last point of blood, start making half circles, looping back and forth, and gradually increase loops into wider spreads as you get farther from your last blood marker. I have picked up blood or tracks by this method. It is possible the deer may start bleeding more, thus enabling you to have a better chance of finding it.

If this doesn't work, try checking creek banks ahead of you. The wounded whitetail, even though it may not have been dripping blood, may do so when it crosses a creek or ditch. Blood will be more likely to drip to the ground when the whitetail goes down the bank rather than going up it.

Any deer trails near your last blood will be worth checking. Don't just look for blood, actually follow each trail a reasonable distance before determining the deer didn't take it. The wounded whitetail has a tendency to use old trails for quick departures.

Figure 18
When all blood and tracks are lost, try the loop method. You can be amazed how new sign may be picked up. Illustration by Larry Smail.

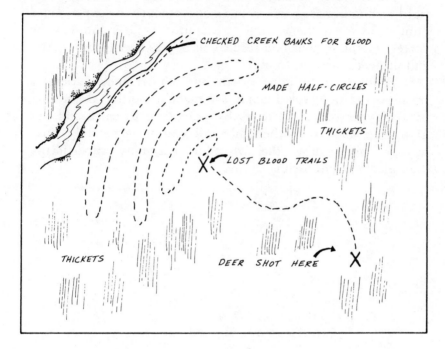

It is also good to check any deer beds you find, to look them over carefully for any blood. When a wounded whitetail beds, it takes but a short time to mat down the brush and leaves, and it is almost certain to leave blood in bed. I have often lost a trail, then found a bloody bed a short distance ahead. If you do locate the bed, be sure not to trample all around it, but try to pick up a new trail leading away from it.

After all methods of trailing are lost, try to locate the whitetail itself. I will discuss a few good methods for attempting to recover a downed whitetail in a later chapter. It is best to trail a whitetail to recover it, and the hunter who just takes off in hopes of spotting a downed deer immediately after it has been shot makes a big mistake. He may get lucky and locate the deer, but he may also walk over valuable sign which could lead to his deer.

Trailing can be fun, exciting, and very rewarding if the right techniques are used. It is a good practice for experienced hunters to teach the younger generation of deer hunters the correct methods. The end result will be less deer left to waste, and protect our right to hunt.

Trailing can be done by anyone who remains patient, a most important factor. Even if you made a poor hit, the trophy of a lifetime could be yours by practicing patience and not giving up. Stay with the trail until you are absolutely sure, beyond any doubt, the whitetail was only superficially wounded and impossible to find.

CHAPTER 9

THE VITAL HITS

I am sure all deer hunters agree that the vital hit constitutes the perfect, naturally desirable shot. The end result is a quick, humane death for the animal, a happy moment for the hunter to know that a deer was killed cleanly and quickly.

Many body areas have a vital spot that brings a quick death for a whitetail. Liver and paunch shots do kill, but they will not be discussed in this chapter. Death may result from a wound in these areas, and some may determine it is a vital hit, but I felt it best to write another chapter on each, since many whitetails hit in the liver or paunch area are lost.

THE BOILER ROOM

The lung and heart area is the most preferred aiming spot, and should be, as a hit by gun or bow usually results in a quick death and an easy recovery. I refer to it as the boiler room, like the engine room of a ship.

As mentioned in Chapter 1, the inflated lungs of an adult whitetail resemble the shape of a football, about nine inches

Figure 19
Illustration by Larry Smail.

in length and six inches in width. Any shot through the shoulders, up to five inches behind, is almost certainly going to hit the lungs.

The adult whitetail heart, about six inches in length and four inches in width, resembles the shape of a grapefruit. The heart lies low in the chest cavity, just above the front leg, and a shot placed just behind or above the front leg will pierce it.

I have seen many different reactions when a whitetail is shot through the heart or lungs. A hit through the heart and lungs alone will usually cause the deer to tear out at a fast speed. The only difference is usually the heart only shot. This whitetail may have a tendency to run erratically and irregularly, even though it may tear off at a fast speed, jump and change direction, with no consistency. The lung shot deer, also at a fast speed, runs a straighter course or may turn a little to the left or right.

The tail of the whitetail most often will drop, but in unusual cases may stay up for 20 or 30 yards. It is rare for the tail to stay up, but there are times when it may go only halfway down and seem to hold that position.

I have heard of cases where a whitetail was shot completely through the vitals and the deer only flinched a little. After a matter of seconds the deer would fall or drop to its knees, but never run. I have never seen this happen, but these tales have been written about by experienced hunters.

How soon the whitetail begins bleeding when hit through the heart or lungs depends on exactly where the shot is placed.

A heart or lung shot deer will usually tear out at a fast speed with the tail tucked. Photo by Leonard Lee Rue III.

The low-hit heart shot will usually begin bleeding within 10 to 20 yards, and in cases where a main artery is hit, bleeding will be almost immediate. The blood color from a heart shot will be crimson red, and often splatter up to a few feet from the trail.

Most heart shot whitetails I have trailed were down in 100 yards or less. I have seen some go for 200 to 300 yards, but these are usually cases where the heart was only nicked. The bullet or arrow that completely penetrates the heart produces an easy blood trail to follow, and an easy recovery.

There has never been a study on how soon the beat will stop in a heart shot whitetail, and I don't believe a study would be feasible from a biological or humane aspect. I feel certain a heart exploded by a bullet will surely stop beating sooner than a heart just nicked. I feel a heart completely penetrated by an arrow will stop beating as quickly as one hit by a bullet.

Many years back, while bow hunting with my dad in eastern Pennsylvania, he managed to hit a small spike buck low, just above the brisket and behind the right front leg. After a one-hour wait, he picked up the easy trail, and began pursuit. Within a few minutes he came upon the buck, bedded down and still alive, with its head up. Dad had no weapon with him so left the buck, assuming he could return in a little while and it would be dead.

When we returned the buck was indeed dead. After noticing an entrance hole at the base of the brisket, we were astonished that the heart could have been missed, and when the deer was gutted, discovered the heart had been sliced along one side. The broadhead had not gone through, but had neatly made an incision along the heart muscle. This buck lived for better than an hour.

I believe that waiting to trail a heart or lung shot whitetail is not a necessity, however a short wait will not hurt. If you give the deer 20 minutes before trailing, it's not going to go anywhere if your hit was perfect. Because of the chance your shot was not as true as assumed, by waiting, you will avoid possibly spooking the deer farther away.

Blood color from the lung shot will be very bright red, almost pink, usually found within 20 yards of the hit. The blood will often start slowly, but continue to increase as the trail progresses, and it never seems difficult to follow. A great deal of blood will smear on high grass or bushes, and it will not spurt far off the trail, as does the heart shot, unless an artery has been severed.

After the lung shot whitetail has gone 40 to 50 yards, it is possible to find blood which appears foamy, caused from the lungs leaking air through the entry or departure hole. I have trailed lung shot whitetails that left foamy patches every time blood was found. The bow hunter who recovers his arrow after a pass-through lung shot may find air bubbles in blood on the arrow shaft, a pleasing sight after an unsure hit. Be sure not to confuse another type of air bubbles in blood, as a whitetail that throws blood while running leaves a slightly bubbly looking trail. The foamy mass of blood from the lung shot is obvious, basically a mass of tiny air bubbles. Larger bubbles do not necessarily relate to the lung hit.

The lung shot whitetail will usually travel at a fast, hard pace, belly low to the ground the first 50 to 60 yards, then usually go into staggers just before going down. If you are close enough it is possible to hear the animal coughing. When the whitetail has both lungs punctured, it will drown in blood as the lungs try to take in air. This doesn't sound humane, but in all actuality death is very quick, taking only a matter of seconds.

Just how far the whitetail travels after being lung shot depends upon several things. First, a whitetail that was aware of the hunter's presence may run harder than one that has no idea what has happened. Another thing, I have found that the higher in the lungs the hit, the further it will go, but the traveling distance difference of the low hit is not substantial. Both hits will put a deer down quickly. I have seen low hit lung shots put a deer down in less than 30 yards, others go up to 150 yards. The average distance is 80 to 100 yards.

For years I wondered if a whitetail could survive when shot through only one lung. I assumed this deer would eventually die, but probably run much farther before going down. While doing research I wrote to qualified biologists for opinions on one lung only shots. Although highly qualified, all were skeptical as there had been no tests done so answers or opinions were not given. I decided to ask Dr. Philip S. Palutsis, physician and surgeon, if he thought a whitetail could survive on only one lung. His answer was, "Any animal, including man, can survive quite nicely on just one lung. In fact, one lung is often removed as a treatment for lung cancer. Therefore, if no major blood vessel is injured in the lung, or if infection does not set in, an animal may live with just one lung."

Now, when I think back to several instances where I assumed that only one lung was severed, I understand why I was not able to recover the deer. To this day, I have recovered only one whitetail hit through the top portion of the right lung. I do not feel this is what killed the deer, as I had also severed the aortic artery along the backbone.

The gun hunter will probably never realize that only one lung is hit. The bow hunter, on the other hand, can sometimes see his angle of shot and the amount of penetration, so has the opportunity to judge whether or not he has hit just one lung. He can then trail the animal accordingly.

Dr. Palutsis stated infection may also set in and cause death, but since this could take a considerable amount of time, the only chance to recover the deer is to take up the trail immediately and push it to produce a greater blood loss. I would trail quietly, staying close enough to keep the whitetail moving.

The lung and heart shot will continue to be the hunter's choice, in most cases a quick death for the whitetail. It provides the largest vital zone of the whitetail's body and provides an easy trail to recovery.

THE KIDNEY SHOT

The egg shaped kidneys of the whitetail lay high, just below the back, slightly in front of the hips, and usually produce one of the quickest kills when punctured. When severed, they can bring a whitetail down even faster than the lung and heart shot. Since

Figure 20
Illustration by Larry Smail.

adult whitetail kidneys measure only about $3^1/2$ x $2^1/2$ inches, they hardly warrant shooting at. In most circumstances kidneys are hit accidentally, or at least we hope so, as anyone who picks them as an aiming point would not act out of common sense.

The kidneys are usually hit when a whitetail is standing broadside, or quartering into in some cases. It is nearly impossible to hit the kidneys when a deer is angling away as the arrow or bullet goes forward of the kidneys, or strikes the hip behind. The hunter who aims for the kidneys when a whitetail is standing broadside passes up a vital zone approximately four to six times larger, the basic size difference between the kidneys and the heart and lungs.

The basic kidney function is to maintain proper water balance, regulate the acid concentration, and excrete metabolic wastes. Many hunters wonder why kidneys are such vital organs, in the sense that they kill so quickly when destroyed. Dr. Palutsis said, "The organ of the body which receives the most amount of blood is the kidney. Therefore, all the body's blood flows through it every minute. When blood loss occurs from the kidney, it can be compared to removing the drain plug from a bathtub." This tells us that the whitetail would have a massive hemorrhage when the kidney is hit.

It would not be unreasonable for a hunter who has hit a deer too far back to hope for the kidney shot instead of the gut shot. More than once I prayed that a poorly aimed shot would hit the kidneys, and any hunter who has seen an arrow pass through the back part of the abdominal cavity can at least hope. Trailing a kidney shot whitetail does not begin to compare with trailing the gut shot whitetail.

When the kidneys are hit, blood color will be crimson red, resembling heart shot blood color. The whitetail will usually start bleeding within 10 yards, and in some cases blood might be found at the hit location. Blood may have a tendency to spurt slightly, so might be along the sides of the trail. The whitetail will bleed a great deal internally, as well as externally.

The blood trail will be easy to follow, even if the intestines are also punctured. The gut shot will sometimes plug the entry or departure hole, but the kidneys are high enough so blockage will not occur, particularly in the entry hole.

A whitetail hit through the kidneys will jump straight up or lunge forward. Running is usually moderate, not at breakneck speed like lung shot cases, and it may even slow to a walk just before going down. I have helped trail several kidney hits, two my own, where I watched the whitetail until it was down. Both slowed to a walk for the last 10 to 15 yards.

Any kidney shot whitetail should be recovered in less than 100 yards, and 50 yards is common. I have never seen one go more than about 75 yards.

Many hunters have taken kidney shot whitetails by gun or bow and never realized it. They usually assume a main artery was hit or the animal just bled out. When your deer is gutted, find the kidneys along the underneath of the back, usually sur-

CAROTID ARTERIES
(JUGULARS)

AORTIC ARTERY

FEMORAL
ARTERIES

HEART

LIVER
(RIGHT SIDE OF THE BODY)

STOMACH

Figure 21
The three major arteries of the whitetail. Illustration by Larry Smail.

rounded by fat and fairly hard to the touch, so you can check them. If they have been punctured by a broadhead, you will be able to tell easily. The bullet-hit kidney is also easy to identify, provided the bullet has not mutilated it.

THE BLOOD VESSELS

There are three major arteries in the whitetail's body, two that I refer to as semi-major, as well as countless smaller blood vessels. The first major artery is the aortic, which comes out of the top chamber of the heart, goes upward, then runs under the spine, practically the entire length of the deer's body. At the

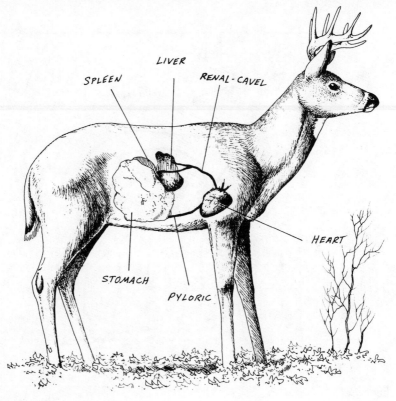

Figure 22
The two semi-major arteries of the whitetail. Illustration by Larry Smail.

point where the hips begin, it forks off and runs down each hip
into the legs. These arteries are called the femorals. Also coming
out of the heart's top chamber are the carotid arteries, also
known as the jugulars. The carotids run forward up to the neck,
along each side of the windpipe, and under the spine. This
completes the major arterial system.

The two semi-major arteries are the pyloric and the renal-
caval. The latter artery comes from the heart's middle chamber
to connect with the spleen and liver, the pyloric from the heart's
lower chamber to connect with the stomach. Both are relatively
short and do not offer much chance of being severed. The

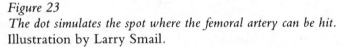

Figure 23
The dot simulates the spot where the femoral artery can be hit.
Illustration by Larry Smail.

diameter of the major arteries is about one-half inch, but the two
semi-major arteries are slightly smaller.

When any of the three major arteries is severed, death
comes quite quickly, especially if the deer is pushed after being
hit, or frightened considerably, such as by eye to eye contact
with the shooter. This causes a more rapid heart rate and induces
faster bleeding.

It has been determined that the whitetail must lose about 30
percent of its blood capacity for death to occur. In the average
adult whitetail this is about 2¹/₂ pints, lost either externally or
internally. The major arteries will cause fast blood loss, but I
believe the pyloric and renal-caval arteries bleed more slowly,
judging from past bow hunting experience, but there have been
no studies done to recognize the total values of these two arter-

Figure 24
The facing away shot offers the best chance of hitting the femoral artery.
Illustration by Larry Smail.

ies. I have noticed on some paunch shot deer that bleeding has
been more severe, compared to others hit in the same general
vicinity, and assume one of the two arteries was severed. I have
seen death come more quickly than paunch shots with a lower
volume blood loss but still would not push this deer in hopes of
a faster recovery. Blood loss might be quickened, but trailing
very difficult because of stomach matter clogging the hole. I
would rather trail this deer 200 to 300 yards after a four to six
hour wait, than trail it several hundred yards further because I
couldn't be patient.

Many times the hunter is not even aware the aortic artery is
severed, particularly if it is through the upper chest cavity. He
assumes it was a lung shot, but many times the artery was hit

and the deer bled out quickly. I have hit the aortic under the spine, when my shot was too far back, and death is usually quick, within 100 to 150 yards. It is generally easy to follow the bright red blood color, true with any major artery hit. I never choose to shoot near the top of the back in hopes of hitting the aortic, a luck type hit not fair to the animal. You stand a better chance of hitting meat along the back than hitting the aortic.

A carotid (jugular) is hit many times because of a missed shot, when the arrow or bullet finds its way into the neck and hits the artery. Some gun hunters will take a neck shot when they are sure of hitting it, but it is risky business for the bow hunter. If you are shooting on level ground at a broadside deer, you are more likely going to hit the windpipe if you also hit the carotid arteries, since they run side by side. If shooting from an elevation, there is a chance of hitting a carotid artery without hitting the windpipe.

When the carotid arteries are severed, you will see a very obvious blood trail, since most of the loss is external. I was amazed at how much blood I saw the first time I trailed a whitetail hit through the jugulars. It may spray several feet to the side as the heart continues to pump. I have seen whitetails go down in 40 yards, and others go 150 yards. This deer should be picked up without any problem. However, it is possible to think you have hit the jugulars when it was only neck muscle, which bleeds heavily at first, but after a couple of hundred yards begins subsiding.

Many hunters nearly kick themselves out of the tree when they aim at the chest and hit the hips, which has happened to me while bow hunting. I have never hit the femoral artery from this shot, but I have helped trail many deer, shot by both gun and bow hunters. This is the kind of shot we are ashamed of, but still it happens, like it or not, so make the best of the situation. Many hunters have lucked out, so to speak, and hit the femoral artery on a trophy buck, which counts in the end.

This shot should not be taken intentionally, but there are two ways the whitetail could stand to let your broadhead or bullet get to the femoral artery, broadside or facing directly away. You have a better chance to hit the femoral artery when facing away than broadside. There are two arteries, one running down each hip. When you shoot at either hip facing away your target will narrow, compared to shooting at the whole hip from a broadside angle, as the artery lies closer to the outside of the hip when the deer is facing away. When broadside, the artery is deeper inside the muscles, requiring more penetration to get to it. The femoral artery lies inward from the leg bone, so you would have to shatter the bone if shooting broadside. Although the artery can be hit more easily from the facing away angle, it is not recommended as there is far greater chance of hitting only muscle. I recommend under all circumstances the hip shot deer be pushed and trailed immediately. This will be discussed again in Chapter 12, "The Non-Vital Hits".

The femoral artery blood trail will be easily seen, as with other major artery hits, but not as well as with the carotid artery hit. Blood may be found at the location where the deer was shot, or close to it. If the deer was hit from the facing away angle, blood will be found near the center of the tracks. The blood may spurt, but will not be as far off of trail as the carotid artery blood. This deer will usually go 80 to 100 yards, but a little farther is not uncommon. You can pretty well bet, if you have trailed the leg-hit deer more than 150 yards, you did not sever the femoral artery.

When any major arteries are hit, whitetails take off with a jump and run, but maybe not as fast as the breakneck speed of the lung shot. The artery hit will slow the deer almost to a walk just before it goes down. It will usually attempt to get to its feet over and over, but will quickly succumb to death.

THE SPINE SHOT

I have seen several spine shot deer, and most were easily recovered. After a spine hit, the animal usually can no longer function or move properly. This hit is one that pleases most hunters, simply because the deer will drop and, in many cases, cannot get back to its feet.

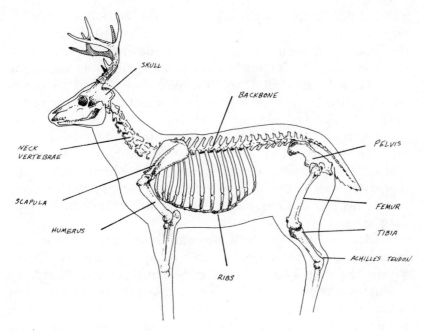

Figure 25
Partial skeletal system of the whitetail. Illustration by Larry Smail.

Two areas of the body where spine damage will occur are along the backbone, from the shoulder to the hip, and the neck vertebrae. Both hits will drop a whitetail instantly, providing the spine is broken. In cases where the backbone is split, the deer will drop, but may get back on its front feet and drag itself. The back legs become useless and will not function.

When hit through the neck and the vertebrae is broken, the whitetail drops and is not able to drag itself as everything is basically paralyzed. The deer will sometimes lie on the ground and quiver, even though it cannot move.

Since the aortic artery runs just underneath the spine, it may be hit when the backbone is hit. It is possible even on the neck shot to hit the carotid arteries or windpipe along with the neck vertebrae, especially if shooting from an elevated stand. If the major arteries are not hit, the animal may have to be shot again through the vitals. I have had to do this on a few occasions, even though it wasn't much fun, but it is the humane thing. I have made a couple of spine shots where the deer was able to crawl 20 to 30 yards before I could get down from my tree. It is best to leave your stand and dispose of the deer immediately.

I know of one whitetail that lived for more than an hour after being spine shot, just in front of the hips. The animal managed to pull itself about 50 yards from where it had originally been shot. A trail is easy to follow from a spine shot deer, mainly because it is moving slowly and there should be obvious drag marks.

Many hunters will be fooled into thinking a spine shot has been made, when the deer has not really been broken down. Whitetails, shot with a gun, may be knocked down and have problems getting to their feet. This is many times the case when it has been hit high, near the loin area. A hunter may begin to climb down from a stand only to have the deer get back on its feet and leave in a hurry. This can leave a hunter scratching his head. Probably the backbone was not broken, only slightly damaged.

THE BRAIN SHOT

The brain is easily hit when a shot is made to the forehead in a case where the whitetail is facing you, less likely from a broadside angle. I know of no hunter who has intentionally tried for a brain shot. It would be pointless, since other vital areas are much larger and offer more room for error.

Although I don't believe I have ever made a brain shot, I have heard of cases. Usually the deer drops in its tracks, thrashes about slightly, and then perishes very quickly.

There are cases where a hunter may think the brain has been damaged, and in reality it has been. I once made a 25 yard shot on a six pointer as it was angling away, walking at a fairly rapid rate. My arrow caught it just behind the right ear and only penetrated a couple of inches. The buck jumped forward and walked in circles around my tree, never in a straight line to leave the area, I am not sure if it suffered brain damage, or temporarily went blind, but I know it was not responding as it should. I climbed down and walked toward the deer, and knew it could hear me because it would turn its head in my direction as I approached. I disposed of the deer, then felt ashamed for the misplaced shot.

I am sure there are many stories about a deer's reaction when hit in the head, although I don't think many hunters enjoy talking about them. It is going to happen now and then, even though not intentional. We must just make the best of this situation.

Figure 26
Illustration by Larry Smail.

LIVER

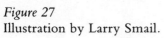

Figure 27
Illustration by Larry Smail.

CHAPTER 10

THE LIVER HIT

*A*lthough the adult whitetail liver is quite large, about 10 by 6 inches, it does not lay at an angle where the complete liver offers a target. It sits somewhat vertically, offering little more to hit than its thickness. There is no gall bladder and the liver's function is to secrete bile that acts in the formation of blood and in the metabolism of carbohydrates, fats, proteins, minerals, and vitamins.

Some think there are cases of liver hits where the whitetail may survive, depending on how solidly the liver is hit. In other words, maybe only an edge slice is not as crucial as a hole completely through. The fact is, bleeding begins the moment the liver is hit, whether it is a slice or a punctured hole. Bleeding may be slower on the slice, but in time increases. I believe all liver hits will kill the whitetail eventually. This will not take days, usually only one to four hours, depending on the severity of the hit. The hunter must use the right techniques and a certain amount of patience to recover the deer.

It is unlikely that a bullet or broadhead will penetrate only the liver, but the paunch, or even a lung, may be severed, depending on the angle of shot. There is a better chance that only the liver will be hit if broadside, however the angling away shot is best. Although you would not necessarily aim for the liver, there is a good chance of hitting it if your shot is too far back.

A whitetail hit through the liver will usually jump and then run. As a rule, it will not run as hard as when lung shot, but usually at a faster rate than a gut shot deer.

The liver shot deer will usually begin bleeding quickly, probably within 20 to 30 yards just to the side of the trail, but blood will not spurt out as when an artery or heart shot is made. With complete penetration, blood will appear on the side of the low hole, or departing hole, if a shot was from an elevated stand position. This is not always the case if the paunch is also severed as the low hole may clog from stomach matter and tissue, not allowing blood to get to the ground. A drop or so may get out, but it will be spaced, particularly if the whitetail is running.

Liver hit blood color will be medium to dark red, never bright red. If bright blood is found you most likely have hit elsewhere, as well as the liver. If you have hit the lungs as well, as in many angling away shots, the blood will be bright. Any time blood color is dark, it emphasizes that the liver or paunch has been hit.

The liver shot whitetail should be given at least one hour, in most cases two hours, before trailing. If you have a problem with waiting because of personal reasons, or if rain threatens I would choose to wait only one hour before beginning to trail. If rain is a possibility, stay where the shot was made and be ready to begin immediate trailing if necessary. If you leave with the intention of coming back in one hour, rain may begin and wash out your trail. With good weather wait at least two hours, to allow plenty of time for the animal to bed down, usually the case with a liver hit.

Your blood trail will be fair on the liver shot, but at times can become difficult to follow. It will usually start with occasional drops, but increase as trailing continues. Most liver shot

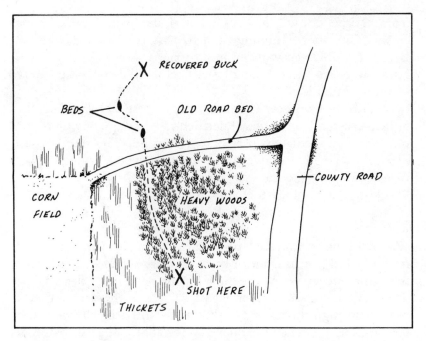

Figure 28
The trail of the liver shot buck. Illustration by Larry Smail.

deer start increasing the volume of lost blood after about 75 to 100 yards, and continue to bleed internally as time goes on, which will soon bring death. There will be no great external blood loss. Before the deer beds down, or perishes, external blood loss will usually start subsiding. When blood suddenly becomes very difficult to find, the whitetail has most likely already bled internally a great deal and is near going down.

One interesting case of a liver shot deer, one year before writing this book, really stands out in my mind, mainly because of the great blood loss.

After a half mile walk on an old road and through a line of thickets, I arrived at my tree stand. I was tying my bow to the hanging string when I heard the deep throated "urps" of a buck in pursuit. Not knowing exactly where the sounds had come from, I knelt down and turned to look behind me. A doe crashed into view, running hard to pass only 10 yards away. Before I could even wonder about what was going on, a small buck came into view about 20 yards behind the doe, desperately trying to catch it.

With the two deer running around close to my stand, the buck consistently grunting, I decided to climb quickly up to the stand and immediately pulled my bow up. The doe was so occupied trying to get away, and the buck so busy trying to play Romeo, neither saw me.

For five minutes they ran by several times, never close enough to chance a running shot. The doe finally ran only 10 yards away and I had the bow up and drawn in one motion. When the buck appeared panting and tongue hanging out, I tried to hold just in front of the shoulders as my 10 yard sight pin came into view. As the buck hit the opening I released, the deer lunged forward, swerved to its left as the arrow disappeared through the left side. I knew instantly the shot was too far back, and watched the buck run for about 50 yards before it was out of view.

Since I was unsure of a liver shot, a gut shot, or both, I decided to stay put for at least an hour, then climbed down, eased over to where the deer was shot, but my arrow was not there. I found blood within five yards of where the deer was hit, silently trailed the buck for about 40 yards, and realized the dark colored blood meant I had most likely hit the liver. I marked the last blood with toilet paper and left. Since darkness was only an hour away, and I was supposed to meet friends, I decided to let the buck go for now.

I arrived back a little after dark with two fellow hunters and lights, picked up the simple to follow trail with blood everywhere along the route. I never had seen so much blood from a liver hit, began suspecting I had possibly caught an artery, but was puzzled since the blood remained dark. After about 150 yards I found a bed with my arrow a foot away, slightly bent and soaked with blood, a large mass of blood in the bed, and a few yards farther another bed in the middle of some thick honeysuckles. As I walked past the second bed I saw the buck, quite dead and considerably stiff. No doubt, he had been dead for some time.

I had never trailed a liver hit deer so easily, blood in great volume all along the trail and the deer had died quickly. Even though more than two hours elapsed since the hit, the amount of stiffness proved it had been dead for some time, 20 to 30 minutes after the shot.

I was able to tell after field dressing that the liver was the only thing hit, a perfect "X" cut through the center. No arteries had been severed, so why was blood so plentiful along the trail, and why did the deer succumb so quickly? "The Waiting Game" chapter told about a fast heart rate increasing blood loss. Since the buck had been chasing a doe, I am sure its heart rate was very high at the moment it was hit, the reason the blood trail was found so quickly, why it left an abundant amount of blood, and why it died so soon. I will probably never see a liver hit whitetail act quite this unusually again, a rare circumstance.

It is common for a liver hit deer to bed down. Almost every time I have trailed one there were one or more beds before I found the deer. Usually they go 150 to 200 yards before they bed down, in some situations not this far. I am sure the deer is feeling quite poorly within a few minutes of the hit and has to bed down for comfort.

If not pushed immediately, a liver hit deer will most often be found a short distance past its bed, or beds. After the deer has bedded, there may not be an existing blood trail where he has left and it can be next to impossible to pick up the departing trail. Do not walk haphazardly around the bed hoping to find an easy trail. Look carefully and patiently, for even if there is no blood, a hoof print may be visible. A main concern is to establish what direction the deer took, and if you have waited the deer out before trailing it should be close by. You should either find a new bed or a dead deer. I know of one liver shot whitetail buck that bedded seven times before we recovered it.

Many hunters claim that a liver hit whitetail will travel a long distance before it goes down, but this isn't so. If pushed, they cover a lot of ground, but if left alone for a couple of hours, a deer will most likely be down in 200 to 300 yards. A deer may go farther, but this doesn't happen often as the liver hit whitetail will bed down as soon as possible.

The shortest distance I ever trailed a liver hit deer was about 80 yards. This deer was left alone all night, after being hit at dusk. The hunter left the area quietly, making sure the deer didn't know he was around. The doe bedded down quickly and was found in its bed the next morning. One liver hit deer went about 400 yards before it was found. The hunter began trailing about 30 minutes after it was shot, and two separate beds found before the deer was recovered indicated the deer was jumped up and pushed.

The liver shot whitetail will die, so don't give up hope in finding it. It may take an extra second effort, a little more patience than other trailing situations, but if you don't hurry, and practice waiting before you trail, this deer should soon be tagged.

CHAPTER 11

TRAILING THE PAUNCH SHOT DEER

*T*he large stomach is a four part organ; the ocumen, reticulum, omasum, and obomasum. Each is a different shape and has its own capacity, and each takes a certain role in the digestive track of the whitetail. The adult whitetail has about 65 feet of intestines.

The classification of a paunch shot deer would include any whitetail hit through the stomach, intestines, or both. It is a hit most hunters hate to see, simply because of the difficulty of recovery. A hunter may shoot at a moving whitetail and hit too far back, or shoot at a quartering-into deer. Although some hunters aim at the middle of the deer, it should never be an emphatic target.

Regardless of how it happens, the bow or gun hunter sooner or later takes up the trail of a gut shot deer. This animal will most likely die, so every effort should be applied when attempting to recover it as many are found simply because a hunter doesn't give up. If you positively know that the deer will indeed die, you may apply yourself with more confidence.

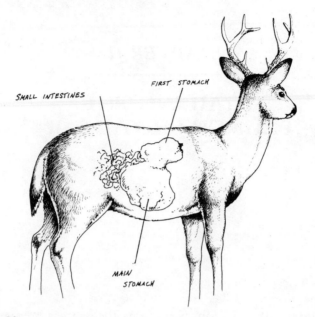

Figure 29
Illustration by Larry Smail.

I was bow hunting at a military base in central Indiana and there was an excellent possibility of getting a deer as the place was loaded with whitetails. After I hunted the better part of the morning, I slipped through a wooded draw and came upon a fellow sitting in a tree. I asked about any action and he told me he had just gut shot a doe. I then asked if he needed help in trailing, but he said he wasn't worried, another deer would probably come along. I couldn't believe anyone could be that atrocious. As far as I know, the guy never even attempted to trail the deer.

Most of the time whitetails react a certain way when gut shot. It is rare for it to leave on a hard run, such as the lung shot deer might do. It may take a couple of leaps, but after jumping will probably just walk off, or may only flinch before walking off. The deer may run slowly for a short distance, but will soon slow to a walk. Basically, any gut shot deer will not leave in a hurry, although fright may change or alter this pattern. Any deer that sees the hunter could leave at a running speed, almost the only circumstance when a paunch shot deer responds this way. The gun hunter may spook the deer more, simply because of the firearm noise.

Pay close attention to how the deer walks off when it leaves, usually in a hunkered-down position. The back will be hunched, its legs generally widespread, the neck stretched out and forward, not upwards as when walking normally.

How long to wait before you begin trailing the paunch shot deer? Most hunters agree about four to six hours. If I shoot a deer through the back portion during the evening, I definitely wait until morning to begin trailing, unless weather is threatening.

Figure 30
The paunch shot deer will walk off with a hunkered-down look. The back will be hunched and the legs somewhat spread apart. Illustration by Larry Smail.

I may decide to come back later that night, but I do not trail immediately unless it is raining or snowing.

If I had to pick a time to shoot a deer through the paunch, I would rather it be in the morning. Then, I can begin trailing after lunch. I prefer this time because of possible frosts or an overnight dew, which can hurt a blood trail.

It is important to let the paunch shot deer go for two reasons. First of all it does not die quickly, it usually takes a few hours before the animal succumbs. If no other vitals are hit, such as the liver or an artery, it will hemorrhage slowly, as well as begin to dehydrate, taking a matter of many hours or even longer.

The next reason is because the whitetail will most always bed down, and thank goodness it does. Imagine trying to trail a wounded whitetail that has been moving around for several hours? It would be next to impossible to recover. The gut shot whitetail will most often bed down soon after it is shot. One small buck lay down only 40 yards from where it was hit, so I stayed in my tree and waited for the next move. After an hour it got back on its feet and walked out of sight, giving me the opportunity to sneak out of my tree and leave. Since I was bow hunting, there was no chance for another shot. Many hunters have watched gut shot whitetails bed down quickly. A friend shot a deer 30 minutes before dark, was unsure of his hit, but since the deer left walking then bedded down only 60 yards away, assumed the arrow had hit the deer too far back. He stayed in his tree until it was dark, then returned the next morning to find the dead deer in the same bed it was in the evening before, hit through the stomach.

Many whitetails will bed down several times. One gut shot buck I trailed bedded down 11 times, which I believe is uncommon. The beds were all within 20 yards of each other so I knew I would find the buck, but it didn't work out that way. The most common number for a whitetail to bed when gut shot is three or four, sometimes fewer and sometimes more, but this is average for those I have trailed.

I am not sure why a whitetail will have so many different beds, usually fairly close together. I don't usually find one bed then another 100 yards away, unless the deer is pushed. I asked a few biologists why a paunch shot deer reacts this way, but there was only speculation. Most felt the deer might be so uncomfortable that it moves to feel better, this doesn't work, so it beds down again. Whatever the reason, look hard to recover the whitetail near the beds.

Many hunters wonder which is most effective, the bullet or broadhead. In regard to the paunch shot, I feel better if it is done

Most always the paunch shot deer will lay down, soon after being hit.
Photo by Leonard Lee Rue III.

by the arrow. I have trailed many paunch shot deer, hit by bow and by gun, and the blood trail seems slightly better with the broadhead, as well as improving the recovery percentage. I have recovered more deer hit through the paunch with an arrow than with a bullet. The better blood trail helps your chances, and the animal is less likely to be spooked by a bow. The deer may go a considerable distance after a gunshot before bedding down.

Although a hunter may hit the stomach and intestines, due to angling shots, there are times when only one or the other is severed. Many hunters wonder which of the two might be most effective. I wasn't able to come up with any answers regarding this, therefore I judge only from past experience. I prefer the stomach hit over the intestinal hit. The stomach shot whitetail usually beds down within 200 to 300 yards, many times closer. The intestinal shot whitetail seems to go farther, and one buck went a half mile before it bedded down. Although we waited about five hours before trailing, we jumped the buck and had to stop. It bedded again about 100 yards from the previous bed and that is where we found it the next day, hit just in front of the hips and an exit out the bottom. I certainly feel the chances of recovery are better with the stomach hit over the intestinal hit.

When trailing the paunch shot whitetail, it is possible to find contents from the stomach or intestines. Although you might have trailed by only blood, there is a possibility that these contents will sooner or later leak out. This material is often found in the beds of a gut shot deer, or on leaves. I once trailed a wounded deer that I didn't realize was gut shot until I found contents in the bed.

Stomach contents are somewhat solid and usually a light tan. Intestine contents are more runny and slimy, a very dark brown or green color. Sometimes a small fleck is all that may be found, but if you detect an odor, it is probably stomach or intestinal matter.

Blood is slow to start on a paunch shot deer, and it is rare to find it close to the spot where the whitetail was shot. Most often it is 40 to 50 yards before blood will get to the ground, in some cases much farther, as it is not uncommon for stomach or intestine particles to clog the hole. Often a bullet or broadhead pulls this matter to the exit hole, filling it in. Since bleeding is much lighter, it may be impossible to find.

On occasion the pyloric or renal-caval artery is hit and the blood trail is better. Although most bleeding occurs internally, some gets to the ground.

The paunch shot deer should be trailed slowly and quietly. I prefer only one other person to help me trail a gut shot deer, with less noise and fewer people messing up what little bit of a trail you might have. Take along a lot of light-colored toilet paper to mark as you will likely lose your trail several times. If blood is only found at several yard intervals, markers will keep you on line and prevent straying off.

The blood trail will probably stay spaced, as well as appear in small drops, sometimes only specks of blood, so two people looking will be better than one. If your deer is walking naturally, it may help you find more blood as the frightened running paunch shot deer will leave a considerable smaller amount of blood.

If you jump the deer, don't trail until you have waited at least one to two more hours. The deer will get farther away if pushed, so if you do not pursue immediately it may bed down again in a short distance.

The gun hunter should watch in front at all times while trailing. Let your partner do most of the trailing so you can be prepared to shoot if necessary. The paunch shot deer will often let the trailer approach very closely before getting up. Sometimes if bedded in thick cover the deer may not get up, even when you are only a few feet away. This is important if you pursue immediately because of threatening weather.

A hit high in the paunch will leave less blood than with a low hit, as a lower hole lets blood leak out more easily. The high hit continues to bleed internally, and sometimes as blood tapers off it is a good sign. The deer has bled internally so not much more is left, and it is often found right after this occurs.

The gut shot whitetail may go to water. Dehydration is a strong factor in the deer shot through the abdomen. Photo by Leonard Lee Rue III.

There is a good chance of having to trail without blood. Unless you have snow on the ground, you may be limited to tracks alone, so pay close attention to the disturbance of leaves. The paunch shot deer seems to walk heavily, because of its hunkered position, and this will help when there is no blood present.

Since you were forced to wait before trailing the paunch shot deer, most blood will have probably dried, much harder to see than wet blood. If ever there is a time to get down on your hands and knees, this is it. You will be surprised how much more blood you can find.

Blood color of the paunch shot deer is very dark red. If you find bright-colored blood, but you hit the paunch area, you can bet you have also hit something else, which is good fortune. It is the stomach or intestine material that causes the blood to appear so dark.

I have seen many paunch shot deer go to water. This happens occasionally on other body hits, but quite often with the gut shot, somewhat of a pattern in my neck of the woods. I am sure there are times this was coincidence, simply because the water hole or stream was in the path, or when a wounded whitetail crossed a body of water in an attempt to lose its pursuer.

After several situations I began to wonder if there was a reason, medically speaking, that provokes a paunch shot whitetail to go to water. Dr. Palutsis replied that, "When a paunch shot deer goes for water, it is a sign of dehydration. An injury, particularly to the intestine, results in much swelling of the intestinal wall. This swelling is from fluid, or water, removed from other parts of the body, and gives the deer a sensation of thirst, for which it seeks water. When a deer, or man for that matter, is shot in the abdomen, and the vital organs, such as the spleen, liver, aorta, are spared, the animal may live for several hours. The most likely cause of death during the first few hours in this case would likely be from dehydration."

My son, at age 13, took his first bow killed whitetail by way of the paunch shot in the early part of the evening. He thought his seven yard shot had missed, and stayed in his blind until dark. He then found the slightly bloody arrow with a little slime on the shaft. Since he was only 300 yards from home, he didn't bother to look for a trail. He assumed some kind of a poor hit, and kept himself from high expectations.

After checking his arrow and realizing he had probably gut shot the doe, I figured we would wait a couple of hours before attempting to take up the trail. There was a chance of rain and I didn't want to leave the deer until morning. However, a vehicle pulled into my driveway and a local hunter asked if either of us had shot a doe that evening. Coming out from his hunt, he found a freshly killed gut shot doe by the edge of a pond. Knowing the pond was only 300 yards from my son's stand, and since we were the only hunters in the area, we knew it had to be his deer.

I have recovered four other gut shot whitetails lying beside waterholes, a few others that passed over water or around the water's edge. I am convinced they went to water because of thirst.

After watching a gut shot deer for one hour, see it rise from its bed and go directly to a pond, I assume the thirst sensation probably doesn't happen immediately. After being shot this deer ran only 50 yards and bedded. It came to its feet after an hour and walked 200 yards to a small pond, where it was found. There were no other beds between the first and the pond, and I am convinced that deer had one thing on its mind—to go for water.

Knowing this can help your chances of recovering a gut shot deer. Even though death does not strike quickly, and there is most likely a slim blood trail, the water hole may be a last hope. After you have trailed the deer as far as possible check any nearby water holes or streams, in or around the water. Don't be satisfied with one quick look as the deer may have drunk, then bedded another 40 to 50 yards away. Check any thick cover by the water, since deer usually choose this to bed down in.

If you are familiar with the area, think out where nearby water is, particularly in the direction the wounded deer has taken. If unfamiliar, a topo map is a great help. All old ponds, drainages, creeks, etc., will be shown. All possibilities are worth checking out.

Even if you don't find the deer at the water hole, there is a chance of finding it along the way. Follow deer trails, preferably if they take you in the general direction of water. You may be fortunate enough to find a new bed, blood spots, any number of things that could help.

The paunch shot deer is most likely a dead one, so handle yourself properly before and after taking up the trail. This deer can be recovered if the proper techniques and patience are used.

CHAPTER 12

THE NON-VITALS

Any hit to the whitetail's body that does not penetrate into the cavity classifies as a non-vital hit. In other words, when no organ or artery is severed, the hit is a superficial wound. This could apply to a leg, bone, muscle or loin hit, basically any wound where blood is present.

Some hunters do not bother trailing a superficially wounded whitetail, which is a poor practice and unethical. Any hunter who abandons a trail, simply because he doesn't feel the hit is serious, has no business hunting. Any whitetail worth shooting at is worth trailing. Just as much effort should be put into an attempt to recover this deer, as into trailing a vitally hit whitetail.

There are hunters who feel a whitetail deer will easily recover if not hit through the body cavity, therefore they do not need to trail it. I know of one hunter who managed to take a doe hit through the top of one ear. Enough blood had been left to make trailing fairly easy, so after stalking the animal to its bed, another well placed arrow did the trick.

As long as there is a blood trail, the deer should be pursued until there is no doubt that the deer has indeed recovered. There is a chance you could be wrong by assuming a hit is only superficial, and there is always the chance of getting a second shot.

Some types of hits can lead to recovery, even though they are not thought of as a vital wound. Being able to recognize the type of wound and how to properly trail it are important factors.

THE LOIN AND BACK HIT

The strip of loin on the whitetail lies just above the kidneys, along the underneath side of the spine, about 10 inches in length. A hit high in the loin may also sever the aortic artery, which will bring the deer down quickly. However, when only the loin is severed it will be difficult to recover.

The loin hit blood color is medium red. Blood usually is seen within 30 to 40 yards of the hit, unless the whitetail is knocked down for a few seconds, then might be found on the spot.

The arrow loin shot will usually produce a better blood trail than the bullet wound, but this does not mean your recovery chances are better. The blood will start slowly, but after 60 to 70 yards the trail will begin to intensify. By the time the deer has run 100 yards, it should become easy to follow. Blood will be found in much greater volume, giving a feeling of great hope, but after the deer has gone 150 to 200 yards, the trail begins to taper off, and shortly after will usually subside altogether.

A deer hit through the back above the spine will resemble a loin shot deer. The blood trail will increase, but will begin to decline after a couple of hundred yards.

The best opportunity to recover the deer is to push it immediately to induce more blood loss externally, helping the trailer to continue. It is unlikely that blood loss from this wound alone will bring the deer down.

The gun hunter, when trailing the loin or back hit whitetail, has great advantage over the bow hunter. By pursuing immediately there will be a chance of a second shot. The trailer should operate alone, or with one other person, trailing quietly and constantly watching ahead.

Figure 31
Illustration by Larry Smail.

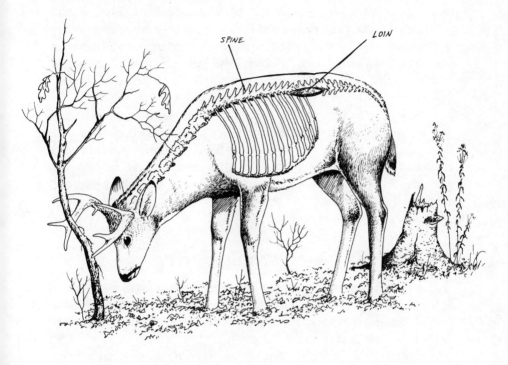

This deer will have a tendency to stop and look back quite often, and stand for a great deal of time while watching its back trail. It is not common for this deer to bed down, however there are a few exceptions. One back shot whitetail bedded down five times before I finally lost the trail and was forced to give up. I jumped it a couple of times and could hear running through thickets ahead of me, but I was never able to see it.

One big mistake that some hunters make is to watch a deer drop, then back off from a second shot. This has happened to me more than once. When a hunter hits a deer high in the back, sees it fall and have a little difficulty getting back up, he presumes a broken spine and decides not to shoot again. Before you know it the deer is up and gone. Although common when gun hunting, it has happened to me during archery season as well. An arrow hit high and too far back, dropping a buck to the ground at dusk. The deer tried for better than a minute to arise, eventually managed to get to its front feet and drag itself into the thickets. I assumed I had broken the spine, but how wrong I was. When I returned later to trail the buck, it jumped up and left the area running fast. I never found the buck.

Many back hits will confuse the hunter into thinking there is a broken spine, so if there is a chance for a second shot, take it.

I have recovered very few deer hit in the back and loin. All you can do is give it your best shot and trail as far as you possibly can. There is a good feeling, however, when you are forced to give up the trail as this deer will most likely recover after a few days of rest.

THE BRISKET AND TALLOW HIT

The gun hunter is somewhat unfortunate and will not know when an area of tallow has been hit, but the bow hunter is often able to retrieve his spent arrow with tallow on the shaft and may be able to tell where it has hit.

Tallow is a white gummy substance, somewhat sticky when rubbed with the fingers. It is usually apparent on the shaft and feathers, or vanes, more so than the broadhead tip. Although you can wipe tallow off the shaft, some greasy substance always remains, and it smears easily.

Tallow is found in three areas of the whitetail's body. One is along the brisket, just under the hide, and running up to the base of the neck. It is also found above the spine, starting at the hips and running about half way along the back towards the shoulders, about 12 inches. A small strip is found under the spine where the hips begin.

The arrow that enters high in the chest cavity and exits through the brisket will show a great deal of tallow on the shaft, with only a few blood spots. Although the arrow is bloody when it begins its exit, the shaft will wipe off blood as it passes through the tallow. One hunter found a couple of specks of blood near the nock end of the shaft, the rest of the arrow almost solid tallow. But the buck was found in 80 yards, as the arrow had entered through the neck and exited through the tallow at the point where the neck joined the shoulders. The carotid artery had been severed, even though little blood was found on the arrow.

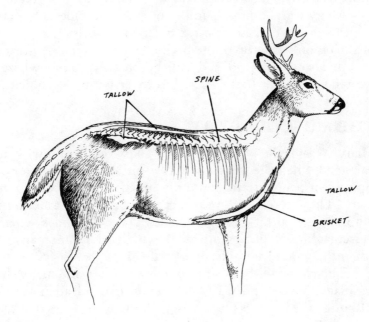

Figure 32
Illustration by Larry Smail.

The arrow that slices only the brisket will show little or no blood on the shaft. Sometimes only one side of the arrow will be tallowy, the other clean. The blood trail will show only a trace of blood and be difficult to follow. If the arrow has failed to penetrate into the chest cavity this whitetail will easily recover. The same goes for the bullet that only scrapes the brisket with no serious damage done. There is a possibility the arrow or bullet penetrated into the chest, and the amount of blood you find while trailing will tell the story.

One disappointing situation is when a bow hunter hits the deer high across the back, then finds only tallow on the arrow shaft with very little blood. I have never recovered a deer hit under these circumstances. Usually only a faint blood trail exists, and it comes to a screeching halt quickly, within 50 to 100 yards. However, I stress that you trail the deer as far as possible, simply because the aortic artery might have been severed.

Many times tallow is found on only one side of the arrow shaft from the high-back hit, similar to the brisket hit, a result of slicing only the top of the back above the spine. A great deal of hair is often cut off and will be on the ground where the whitetail was hit. This deer will recover with no problem.

THE MUSCULAR HIT

Many areas of the whitetail's body allow only the muscle to be damaged when the arrow or bullet hits. It may be due to the amount of penetration, or simply because there is only muscle there. These so called "meat hits" can often fool a hunter into thinking a vital hit has been made. There are times when the muscular hit will put a whitetail down, but there are many times when the wound will be superficial.

The whitetail shoulder is extremely tough and many shoulder blades have stopped a swift moving arrow dead in its tracks. Although the bullet is rarely stopped, there are times that the hit is too low or too high.

When the bow hunter recovers his arrow after a shoulder hit, many times there will be blood only two or three inches up the shaft, indicating very little penetration. The more pounds pushing the arrow, the better chance of penetration. I have hit whitetails through the center of the shoulder blade, cracked it open, and gone through to the opposite side, hitting both lungs in the process. I shoot about 65 pounds with a 2117 shaft. But there have been times when I have shot a little too far forward and hit the deer in the shoulder joint, which will usually stop almost any arrow. The end result is a flesh wound to the muscle, and this whitetail will usually begin bleeding within 30 to 40

Figure 33
Most "meat hits" are usually only superficial wounds, with the exception of the rump. Illustration by Larry Smail.

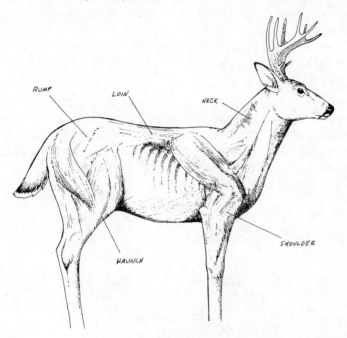

yards. The blood trail will increase until the deer has gone about 100 yards, then taper off and soon stop completely. The blood color will be a bright red, as it is with all meat hits.

I have never recovered a whitetail hit in the shoulder with only a couple of inches of penetration. This is no more than a flesh wound and the deer will easily recover.

Many times the gun or bow hunter will hit the neck muscle and nothing more. Even though the vital spine, windpipe, and carotid arteries are located in the neck, a shot placed too low or too high will hit nothing more than meat.

At times the neck hit whitetail may drop from a bullet, even though the vitals are not touched. The neck muscle arrow will not usually cause the deer to drop. Even if the deer does drop its head or body to the ground, if the spine is not broken it usually will be back on its feet quickly. I have seen neck hit whitetails have trouble holding the head up after being hit. The head seemed to sway from side to side as they ran off, even though the vitals in the neck were not touched. I assume this to be from severe muscle damage.

The bright red blood trail of the neck hit will usually begin within 20 to 30 yards, or if the deer dropped, blood might be found at the location of the hit. The blood trail will sometimes be in the center of the trail, not to the sides. When the carotid artery is severed, the blood usually sprays somewhat and won't be found in the center of the trail. When you have trailed a neck hit whitetail for 75 yards or more, and there is no blood sprayed to the sides, no air bubbles indicating a severed windpipe, then you can bet only muscle was damaged.

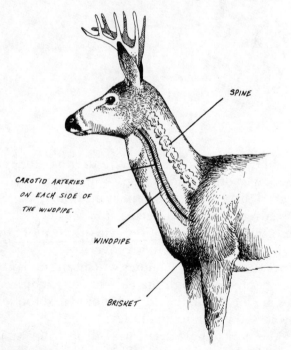

Figure 34
A hit too high or too low may miss the vitals and hit only the neck muscles.
Illustration by Larry Smail.

The blood trail will increase in volume, but it will not subside as quickly as the shoulder hit deer. I have trailed some neck hit deer for 200 yards, and found more blood than I did at 100 yards. The neck hit deer bleeds well as a rule, but it will lessen after 250 to 300 yards, depending on how much muscle was torn. I have found the arrow neck shot bleeds a little better than the bullet wound, particularly if there is an exit hole out of the opposite side.

The best opportunity for recovery is to trail the deer quietly and immediately. There is a chance that pushing will keep the wound bleeding, allowing time for you to spot the animal and shoot again. It is unlikely a non-vital neck hit will bring the deer down from loss of blood, but the deer may bed down allowing you to get up on it if you have trailed quietly and cautiously.

Like many meat hits, the neck shot deer will probably recover. In a few days this wound will be healing and the deer back to normal. Keep in mind, even though the neck hit may bleed profusely at times, this does not mean the animal will die.

THE HIP SHOT

As mentioned in a previous chapter, this shot is usually one we are ashamed of, but once it happens we must trail the deer and handle it properly. It is difficult to roll into a check-in station with a trophy buck that has a hole in the rump. You feel like everyone is talking about you, but almost anyone who has hunted deer for several years, either with bow or gun, has at one time or another hit a deer in the hips.

There is always hope the femoral artery is severed, but most often it is not. This leaves nothing but a solid mass of damaged muscle, but this whitetail can be recovered. I have recovered many whitetails shot through the hips, even when the femoral artery was missed. One bow hunter claims he recovered almost every whitetail he helped trail that was shot through the hips. He stated that he might start aiming for the back end of the deer, but hopefully he was joking.

Why is the recovery rate of both arrow and bullet wounds to the hips so good? I believe it is due to extreme destructive muscle damage. Some whitetails have a difficult time using one of the back legs when it is hit with a great deal of penetration. I have seen the back end completely drop to the ground when hit, and many times they show difficulty in trying to run.

The hip shot deer should be pushed immediately, whether hunting with bow or gun. It is not necessarily for the intention of getting a second shot, but the idea is to push the deer to keep it bleeding and to hopefully cause further damage.

Like all other meat hits the blood color is bright red. You can usually find blood close to the spot where the deer was hit and it will usually intensify as you continue pushing. Bleeding is good, so don't be fooled into thinking the femoral artery is severed. Blood may be found right in the tracks, since a great deal will run down the leg. As the deer moves its hips, it will throw blood outwardly, so it will also be found to the sides of the trail.

The hip shot whitetail is likely to bed down if you are not close in pursuit. I have often heard the hip shot deer ahead as it tried to get out of bed. If you are fortunate, you might have the opportunity for another shot. Often the second shot takes the hip shot deer.

I am not sure which is more damaging, the facing-away hip shot, or the broadside hip shot. Both do a great deal of harm.

I had a small buck come within 15 yards of my stand one evening, about an hour before dark. The deer stuck around but never seemed to offer a good shot. Bow hunting, I was forced to wait until the deer turned broadside. It managed to quarter away a little more than I wanted, but I decided to take it and I assumed the arrow caught it square in the left hip, but it turned and ran easily, as if there were nothing wrong.

I decided not to trail immediately, since I was unsure of my hit. After a 30 minute wait, with darkness approaching, I found an easy to follow blood trail. It seemed to keep getting better so I decided to stay with it, and after about 150 yards I heard a limb pop up ahead. I eased along, spotted the buck bedded only 20 yards in front of me, trying desperately to get to its feet, but unable to do so. The back end was damaged so severely that it was unable to put weight on the legs. Another well placed arrow did the job.

This was a typical hip shot deer. I have seen some go 200 to 300 yards before bedding, but most will do so even sooner. Some hip shot whitetails were dead when found, others had to be disposed of.

The hip shot deer can be recovered under the right circumstances. If the arrow or bullet has penetrated deeply enough, the deer is in a big heap of trouble. Along with severe hemorrhaging, there is a great deal of muscle damage.

THE HEAD SHOT

Just like the hip shot, this is another disappointing and embarrassing situation. Although the brain is most likely hit from the facing-into shot, it is less likely to be hit from the broadside shot, particularly by the bow hunter.

I have only made two head shots on whitetails (thank goodness) since I began deer hunting, and neither hit the brain. Once a small buck entered an area of thickets only 20 yards from my stand, turned broadside and stopped as if to say, "Here I am. Shoot me if you can!" I wasted no time coming to full draw, settled my sight pin on the chest and just as I was about to release, a vehicle rounded a corner on a nearby gravel road and the horn honked twice. The buck lunged forward, I flinched and the arrow caught it just below the base of the antler and above the ear. I could see my arrow sticking out of the deer's head as it ran off, and it rattled every time it hit brush.

I followed the blood trail for about 100 yards before it finally subsided. I recovered most of my arrow, but the business end of the shaft was evidently still in the deer's skull. This bothered me, and not until the first day of gun season did I know what happened to the buck. I ran into a 12 year old boy who killed the buck only a quarter mile from where I had originally hit him. The broadhead was not embedded in the deer's skull, but there was a nice scab over the spot where the broadhead had hit. The boy said the four pointer had acted normally as it approached his stand, so the deer had recovered.

I have heard of other situations where embedded broadheads have been found in the skull, and have seen some photos. But every case indicated that the deer acted perfectly normal before it was killed. I believe a head shot either drops the deer in its tracks, or the animal eventually recovers. If the brain is hit, the deer usually drops immediately. If the deer leaves running, it will most likely recover. I am sure there are exceptions, but most of the time this is the end result.

No one takes a head shot intentionally, but like the hip shot it will occur. The good thing is, the deer either dies quickly or recovers. These circumstances are, fortunately, rare. I can count on one hand the number of head shots that have been made by myself or companions in 25 years of bow and gun hunting.

As long as we deer hunt and practice taking only good shots at vital areas, only on occasion will we hit the non-vitals. The largest percentage of shots taken will be in the right places. If we take unwarranted shots, we jeopardize our personal values, as well as our hunting heritage.

CHAPTER 13

THE STRING TRACKER

Bow hunters have often wished there was a string attached from the implanted arrow to the hunting bow, particularly when a poor hit was made. It would seem as though it would be a great advantage for the trailer. Imagine spending several hours of frustrating trailing vs. following a string directly to it. There is no doubt it would simplify trailing significantly.

I am sure many bow hunters are not aware of a string tracking device and others have heard of this development but were afraid to try it.

This chapter will explain the string tracker, its abilities, the pros and the cons. After you have achieved a better overall knowledge of the string tracker, decide whether or not it is meant for you.

The string tracking device I tested is "The Game Tracker", manufactured in Flushing, Michigan. It consists of a black canister designed to screw into the bow handle and a spool of line inserted into the canister. A snap-on lid over the canister's end has an opening that allows the line to come out and attach to the business end of the arrow. A small wire loop is furnished to attach between the broadhead and the shaft. As the screw-in broadhead tightens, the loop will tighten, so the string can be attached.

The model 1500 Game Tracker that I tested comes with 1250 feet of line. A stick-on piece of plastic that caps over the spool allows you to see how much line has been taken out. The 22 pound nylon test line is white, presenting an easy to follow pattern.

It is recommended to pull a few inches of line out to be sure it is moving freely. I have never had any line hang-up, but it is a good precautionary move. Unless the line comes out easily, it would drastically affect arrow flight.

When I first used the Game Tracker, I thought it best to test shoot at distances of 10, 15, 20, 25, and 30 yards, as I was concerned about any arrow drag that might cause a drop. Here are my results: at 10 yards, no drop; 15 yards, 2 to 3 inch drop; 20 yards, 4 inch drop; 25 yards, 5 inch drop; and 30 yards, 7 to 8 inch drop. I was shooting a Jennings Compound set at 62 pounds, using 2117 shafts, with five inch vanes.

I felt good about the results. The arrow drop increased only one inch per five yards, from 15 to 25 yards. Since my shooting range is usually 20 yards or less, an occasional 25 yards, I felt confident that the slight drop could be easily overcome. If you suspect your arrow drops four inches at a particular distance, simply come up with your aiming point. If you are using sight pins, lower your pin to compensate for the droppage. Although I had a considerably larger drop at 30 yards, I don't usually take these shots, therefore I won't be affected.

It is important for each individual to test archery equipment before actually shooting at a live animal. Although your droppage may not be as severe as mine, most likely each person will experience different results.

I had tested the Game Tracker on level ground, but also shot from an elevated tree stand with similar results, although droppage averaged a little less than shooting on flat ground. If you are going to use the string tracker from an elevated position, definitely test it in that manner. If you use a sight, adjust your pins accordingly.

The assembled Game Tracker ready for use.

When the testing was over and it was time to use the tracker on the real thing, I found it best to tape and secure the line to the end of the shaft as well, a precautionary measure. A broadhead can unscrew as an animal carries the arrow for a long distance, so the tape will still hold the string even though it has slipped off at the broadhead.

One nice thing about shooting from an elevated stand with a string tracker is that you don't normally have to climb down to see if you have missed. If your line rapidly begins pulling out, you can bet you have made a hit. If not, pull on your line to be sure of arrow placement, or simply cut it off and reattach to another arrow. You are unlikely to lose a valuable arrow.

Although the string tracker can be used in hunting small game, I have found it hard to beat on big game. My first experience was several years ago on a black bear hunt in Ontario, Canada. After sitting in a stand for over four hours one evening,

I had a nice blackie approach my bait. It had come from my backside, and was about to walk by when I came to full draw. With the bruin only 15 yards away, I drew and released, but it was obvious my shot was low. The bear gave a "woof", turned, and left the way it had come. I decided to blame the string tracker for missing, silently cursed it and swore I would never use it again, even though I was busy tying more line onto a new arrow.

Within 10 minutes the bear casually strolled back to the bait. Once again it stopped at 15 yards and I wasted no time in drawing down. Within seconds the bear was off and running. Soon all was quiet and I knew the bear was down. There is something great about seeing your line peel out rapidly and suddenly come to a halt.

The string tracker is probably more popular in hunting whitetails than any other big game animal, simply because there are far more deer hunters. Many bow hunting experts have recommended the string tracker after several years of field testing. One well-known hunter from my area told me the string tracker enabled him to recover a fine eight point buck. He had been hunting an old strip mine area of southern Indiana when a doe slowly approached his stand, another deer about 50 yards behind. Although he would have been content to take the doe, he knew there was a possibility of a buck following, but it turned out to be a fawn. Discouraged, he had hung his bow when some white popped into view, a buck with a nice rack tagging up the rear. The hunter glanced at his string tracker, saw everything was set, and released as the buck walked by at only 18 yards. He shrugged when he noticed the arrow sticking in the left side of the buck, several inches behind the chest cavity, knew he had made a gut shot, and hoped the string tracker would do the job. For 15 minutes the string unraveled slowly, usually a few inches at a time, so it was apparent the buck was walking, then stopping. When the line finally halted, it appeared as though 800 feet of line was gone. Since darkness was near, he left the bow hanging in the tree overnight.

At daylight he noticed his line was still attached and sighed with relief. After checking the spool, he saw another 200 feet or more had come out overnight, which meant the buck had moved. But, since the line was still attached, was it possible the buck was lying at the opposite end? He quickly followed the line for almost 300 yards, found a bed that had blood in it, and the line continued onward. He noticed only occasional blood drops, not an easy trail to follow by blood alone. After another 50 yards, another bed with blood spots, and again the string continued. He followed for another 30 yards only to hit a large mass of thick saplings, where the line twisted and turned at different angles, as though the buck was looking for a place to bed down. There was no blood to be seen and his heart sank as he found his arrow at the end of the line, with no buck attached.

He knew the basic direction the buck had been taking and began making circles in front of the spent line. After searching for an hour, almost ready to give up, he spotted something white and the dead buck was only 100 yards from where the string trail ended.

He noticed the entrance hole was clogged with intestinal matter and there was no apparent blood trail. Although the string did not lead directly to the buck, it is obvious this deer might never have been found under normal trailing conditions.

It is sometimes necessary to leave your string tracker and bow behind, especially when you are unsure of your hit. I always carry a few pieces of orange ribbon, cut in strips of about 12 inches, to tie to the string next to the canister. As soon as I have made a hit and the line comes to a halt, I tie an orange bow onto the string. If I stay put and the line starts moving, I am ready to tie on another as soon as the line stops.

When I leave and return later, the first thing I notice is whether or not the ribbon is gone. If more line was taken out and I find my ribbon about 100 yards from where my bow was left hanging, I know the deer went 100 yards while I was gone.

Bright colored ribbons are easy to spot when you are following your line. I have found that surveyor's tape works fine, is easy to tear into strips and shows up quite well.

Although only one line goes out when you have made a hit, two lines are present if you have shot completely through the animal, providing your arrow exits completely. If your arrow passed through and stuck in the ground, two lines appear as the line actually feeds through the hole in the animal, creating a double-line trail.

The bow hunter should be aware that walking around with a nocked arrow attached to the string tracker is a poor practice. Every time the line catches on brush it pulls out more line. This can be prevented by lifting up the canister lid and snapping it down over part of the loose line. I always do this when walking to and from my stand. I believe that raveled line is the main reason for breakage. If the line becomes raveled, I cut it off and dispose of it. It isn't worth the risk of a line breaking as the wounded animal takes it out. Lines break on occasion, many times because of the double trail caused from the complete pass-through. Since there are two trails, it is easier for the line to become tangled, causing it to catch on brush or other obstacles. I am sure thorns and briars play hard against the peeling out line, also.

A minor drawback to the string tracker is a slight noise as the line comes out of the canister when the arrow is released. This is mainly due to the spool being loose, and cotton can be stuffed around the sides to eliminate some of the noise.

An advantage to the string tracker is to keep from getting lost. If you have trailed an animal for a considerable distance, the line will lead you back to where you started. I used the tracker on one occasion for this purpose. I was bear hunting in Ontario in unfamiliar territory, the kind that looks exactly the same each 100 yards. It was very thick and there were no land markers to follow. A friend had hit a blackie the evening before, and even though he had not used a string tracker I decided to bring mine. I tied it where we began trailing and peeled it out as we went along. We trailed the bear about 400 yards, lost it, but found it nice to follow the line back to where we had started. The last thing I wanted was to spend a day or two wandering around in black fly, mosquito infested bush.

The bow hunter should always attempt to recover any line that has been pulled out as it is just plain sloppy to leave line through a hunting area. It will take a long time for line left in the woods to deteriorate.

To think the string tracker should do all of the work is poor logic. A bow hunter must continue to adhere to yardage limitations and not take long-range shots that would not have been taken without a string tracker. Under reasonable yardage, if the hunter tests the device first, he can adjust the sights accordingly. The hunter is supposed to make a good clean kill, so it is foolish to take a poor angled shot because you happen to be using a string tracker. The tracker is only there to help in chances of recovery.

Although I found the string tracker a great advantage when deer hunting, it has become my number one piece of equipment when I go black bear hunting. Since all of my bear hunting is over baits, and shooting is at close yardage only, the string tracker is hard to beat. I strongly recommend it for anyone who has black bear hunting plans. It is common to end up with a poor blood trail when you hit a black bear, mainly because of the thick hide. The string tracker will definitely help even things up.

Although I plan on testing the string tracker even more, I am satisfied that it is an advantage to the bow hunter. It can only help in chances of recovery, and if properly tested, you will be satisfied with its performance.

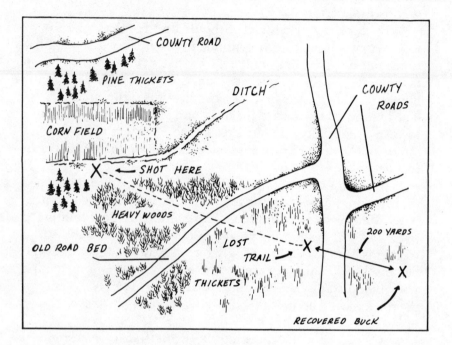

Figure 35
Case #1 - Paunch shot buck of a bow hunter.
Illustration by Larry Smail.

CHAPTER 14

TRAILING INCIDENTS

Thus far we have noted practically every location that could have possibly been wounded in the whitetail's body. We have discussed the most probable reactions of the deer as well as the hunter's "should be" reaction. However, the unexpected will surely happen.

Records of my trailing experiences have become very valuable, simply because they offer advice and reference. I have picked out several incidents for this chapter, many quite common, but educational for future trailing.

Case #1

My good friend Woody Williams shot a decent buck low and too far back early one morning, about the third week of our local archery season. Knowing it was gut shot, he quietly left the area, making sure not to spook the deer if it was bedded close by.

About four hours later I received a call from Woody and agreed to help, along with a couple of others. We began trailing about six hours after the buck had been hit.

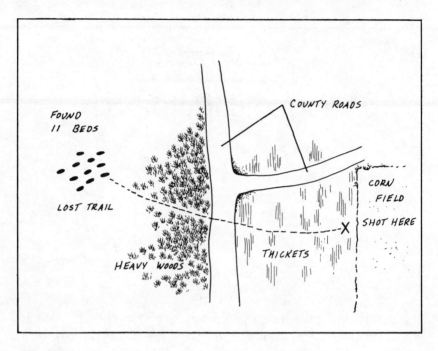

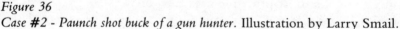

Figure 36
Case #2 - Paunch shot buck of a gun hunter. Illustration by Larry Smail.

We picked up the blood trail just past a small cornfield where the buck was hit. The deer was only walking, every few yards dripping one or two drops of dark blood which matched that on the found arrow. The bloody shaft was only blotched, as to be expected from a gut shot.

We slowly trailed through a small woods, across an old road bed, and when the buck finally hit thickets had hopes it would bed down. But it took the rest of the afternoon to finally trail the buck to a county road.

We searched along the road for nearly 30 minutes, unable to find the trail. The area was a large mass of dense cover, and once again we hoped the deer would bed. I decided to pick up a couple of deer runs leading into the thickets, hoping to find a spot of blood. After more than 100 yards into thick cover, about to turn back, I heard a rustle and about 40 yards in front of me saw a whitetail slowly moving away. As it went through an opening I spotted the antlers, head low, and the deer did not move quickly, like a jumped whitetail should.

I realized it had to be the buck we were after, mentally marked the last spot I saw it and quietly retreated to inform the others. Woody felt we should call off trailing for now. It was getting late and it was apparent the buck had bedded for the first time, hopefully to do so again if left alone.

The next morning we went directly to where I had last seen the buck, but found no blood in a couple of hours. Our only hope was to spread out and comb the area, but no one found anything. We were waiting for Woody to return when he started hollering. We knew he had found it.

The buck had a nice eight point rack and field dressed around 150 pounds. Woody found it inside of a thick, tall, honeysuckle patch. His determination had recovered this buck which had gone only a little more than a half mile, but over 30 hours elapsed until it was recovered. The arrow had entered in front of the hips and exited through the bottom near the penis.

Case #2

It was the first evening of Indiana's gun season following a fruitless morning. I was perched in a tree about 50 yards from a picked cornfield that deer came to frequently, in one of those weather-perfect evenings. A doe came into view about 80 yards up the hill, closely followed by two fawns, and a short distance behind was a small buck.

It was apparent the deer were not going to come closer so I decided to shoot and trust my slug gun. As it roared the buck ducked over the top of the hill, showed no indication of being hit, and I remained in my blind for the rest of the evening. When darkness was near I decided to look, could find no blood and was unsure of the exact location where the buck was standing when I shot.

The next morning I decided on another look, not satisfied that I had missed. I found blood almost immediately after following a set of tracks, proving what a difference a little light can make. I followed a meager dark blood trail for the rest of the morning until it reached a county road. I felt it was a gut shot, decided to get some help, and returned soon with a couple of others to pick up the trail across the road. The buck led us through heavy woods and into an area of thickets. We quickly lost the blood, as though the deer had gone straight up. Although the trail had been slow, blood had been dripping well enough from the walking buck to be followed without any problem.

As we looked high and low, one of my companions finally whistled after locating a bloody bed about 75 yards into the thickets. Although we could not find a blood trail, we found another bed a few yards from the last and soon began finding beds everywhere. We counted 11 beds, but no buck in any of them. After spending the rest of the afternoon scanning the area, I was finally forced to give up.

The buck had gone about 500 yards, there was intestinal material in the beds, so there was no doubt the deer had been gut shot. Why did the buck bed down 11 times, all within a 50 yard radius? Why was there no trail leaving the beds, and why was the buck not found? I would have bet after the first couple of beds that this buck would soon be found. I could better understand this if I had not been so sure of it being a gut shot.

Case #3

It was all but dark when I shot the doe. The arrow seemed to hit a little high and maybe a little too far back. The doe dug out like a vitally-hit deer often does, running as fast as it could. There was hope that my hit was a good one, but somehow I knew better.

With rain forecast, I returned with my dad and another friend about one hour later to begin trailing. The doe had evidently packed the arrow off, so this gave me no evidence to examine. Blood was found a few yards from where the doe

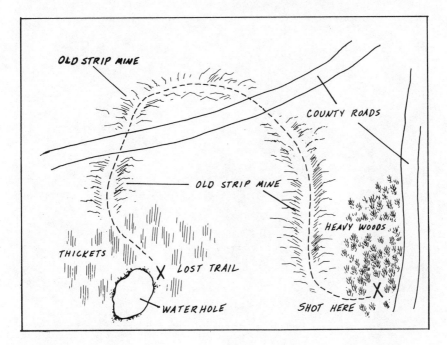

Figure 37
Case #3 - Loin shot doe of a bow hunter. Illustration by Larry Smail.

was hit, a bright to medium red and lots of it, so I presumed I had hit the vitals or had made a meat hit.

We trailed at a fast pace and wasted no time covering the first couple of hundred yards. I knew then the hit was not in the vitals as the deer was bleeding out of both sides. I assumed the hit was high in the back, probably just behind the diaphragm.

After trailing another couple of hundred yards, I ran into an area where blood was everywhere in about a 30 yard circle, on the ground, on bushes, trees, you name it. I decided the doe tried to get the arrow out.

I picked up its departing trail but never found the arrow, although I am sure the doe must have flipped it. The blood trail lost momentum slightly, but still remained easy to follow until

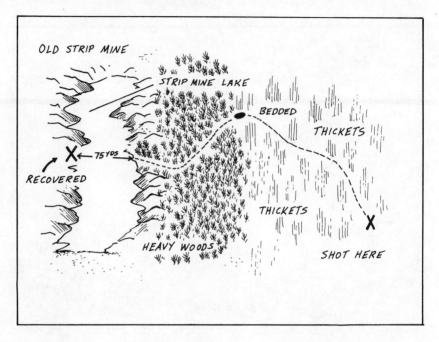

it led us into an old strip mine area grown over with tall pines and brush. We trailed through a half mile of these strip mines when we decided to call it quits at midnight. We had trailed for 5½ hours and realized we had fighting-mad wives to deal with when we got home.

At daybreak I picked up my marker and resumed trailing, but it was two hours before I found a bed. This inspired me, but not to the point that I knew I would recover the doe. The blood trail was dry so I knew I had not jumped the doe, which had evidently bedded here sometime in the night.

I trailed until 1 p.m. then I stopped for a break. It had circled and crossed the road I was parked on, so I marked the spot, went to the truck for lunch, and resumed trailing by 2. The trail tapered off, but there was still blood to follow.

By 4 I found a new bed, this time with blood leaving it. I managed to stay on the trail the rest of the evening, and although I lost blood several times, I always seemed to pick it up again. Just before dark it led to a half acre pond where tracks seemed to stop at the water's edge, no blood to be found, and it had evidently gone in the water. I spent the last few minutes of daylight circling the pond, hoping to find where it came out, but there was nothing. At dark I gave up and called it a day. It was over.

There was no doubt in my mind the wound was only superficial. Even though I might have found a new blood trail the next day, I felt certain this deer would recover. I believe it went into the waterhole in an attempt to lose me, and did. The doe covered about three miles, $1^1/_2$ in one direction before circling back to near where it was shot. I spent a total of $16^1/_2$ hours trailing over the previous 24 hour period. I am still puzzled as to the exact location of the hit. The blood trail was good for a long distance, unlike most loin hits, and the blood never stopped until the doe entered the pond.

Case #4

Another hunting friend for several years, Tom Hodges, arrowed a small buck one evening only a short distance behind his home. The angling away shot caught the deer in part of the hip and angled into the paunch. Tom made an attempt to recover the buck that night, but decided to give up after hearing a running deer ahead in the dark.

He called me and another friend to see if we could trail the buck the next morning. Tom is a teacher and it was impossible for him to get off work. About 7 we found Tom's last blood marker and trailed the buck to a bed, probably where Tom had jumped it the evening before. The blood became spaced since the buck was running, creating a problem to trail for the next couple hours. We would lose it, but then pick it up again. The blood was a bright red, probably the result of the hip wound. We hoped that after Tom jumped the buck, it went only a short distance and bedded down again, but it didn't work out that

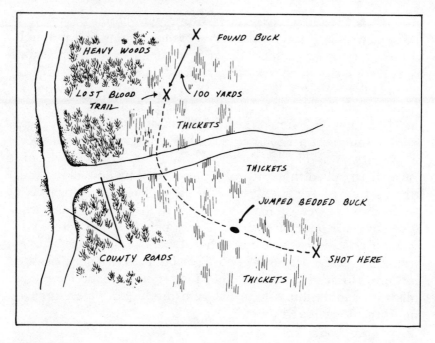

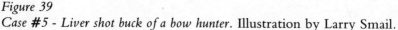

Figure 39
Case #5 - Liver shot buck of a bow hunter. Illustration by Larry Smail.

way. The trail, after about one third of a mile, halted us at the edge of a deep strip mine lake, a pit about 75 yards across and nearly a mile long. It was obvious the buck had jumped in as tracks and blood stopped at the edge, and there was no other explanation. With the water very cold, probably 30 feet deep, we were forced to quit and mark the spot. Tom would soon be home and we would let him decide what to do next.

Tom managed to get a boat into the pit a short distance from his home, followed the opposite bank hoping to find blood, and found the buck lying partially under water with its head resting by the edge, almost straight across from where it had entered the water.

Tom noticed his arrow had entered the left hip and went into the paunch of the five pointer. Since the buck died just before reaching the opposite bank, we assume the swimming might have prompted death. The heart rate probably increased from the swim, causing a faster blood loss. Had this buck gone 100 yards past the water's edge, it might never have been recovered.

Case #5

This is probably a typical liver shot deer situation. I shot a buck in the early morning, the arrow entered a little too far back and I knew it hit either the liver, paunch, or both. I climbed out of my tree and left quietly.

When I returned three hours later with a couple of others, I hoped the arrow had done its job. We found dark red blood within 20 yards, and my arrow where the shot was made. We trailed for about 300 yards when one of the others saw the buck up ahead, walking straight away with head hung low. We marked the spot and took a break, in hopes the buck would bed down again.

When we returned to pick up the trail, we had no trouble until the buck crossed a county road. About 50 yards beyond the blood simply stopped and in the next hour no blood could be found. I decided to venture a little farther, and about 100 yards from the last blood found the four pointer under a shady oak tree, on its belly with head tucked between its front legs, facing the direction from which it had come.

The way the buck was bedded indicated it intended to watch the backtrail, since most dead deer are stretched out on their side. The buck's liver was sliced on the edge and the stomach severed. I am not sure if this is why the buck lived longer than most liver shot deer, but it is one to remember.

Case #6

My dad selected a large maple tree, about 40 yards out in a picked cornfield, in which to perch himself for the evening. A decent buck jumped the barbed fence at dusk, and entered the cornfield. Dad watched for a few minutes, then decided to take a 30 yard shot as it was obvious the buck was not going to come

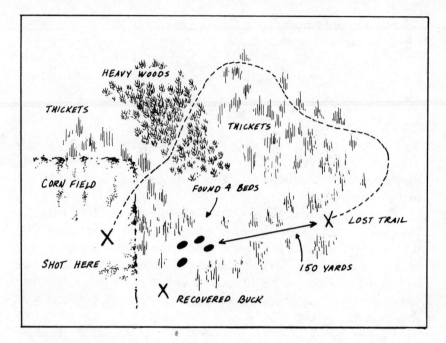

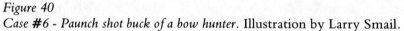

Figure 40
Case #6 - Paunch shot buck of a bow hunter. Illustration by Larry Smail.

closer and darkness was approaching. After the shot the buck
turned and loped back into the thickets. Since the deer appeared
to be somewhat hunkered down, Dad assumed he had scored a
gut shot.

He retrieved the arrow, sprinkled with dark blood, just
past where the buck was standing, and it had completely penetrated. Rain threatened so he found a friend nearby who would
help.

The dark blood trail, unlike most paunch shots, was easy to
follow through the picked cornfield. They found where the
buck jumped the fence and headed back into the thickets, and
for the next 100 yards the trailing remained easy. Then blood
seemed to almost stop, and although they lost the trail several
times, always managed to relocate it. About 11 p.m. they finally

were forced to give up as the trail was lost and they must wait until daylight to resume.

I returned with Dad the next morning and we lucked out. The rain had held off, we picked up the blood trail within 30 minutes and advanced at a very slow pace for the next two hours. Many times we got on hands and knees to find specks of blood and kept hoping the buck had bedded just ahead.

In another hour we lost the trail altogether, tried to follow tracks, but this didn't work either. We knew the buck was circling back, heading directly for the cornfield, so decided to comb the area ahead in hopes of spotting the downed buck.

About 150 yards from where we had lost the trail, I spotted a bed in a high broom sage thicket, bent down to check and found blood. I called Dad, we patted each other on the back and in a few steps found another bed, then another, four beds in all with blood. Just past the fourth bed, Dad took off in a hurry and there was the buck.

The arrow entered about four inches from the underneath side and exited out the bottom, with only the stomach severed. The eight pointer, field dressed at 140 pounds, had covered a half mile and ended up within 200 yards of where it was shot. Although the buck went a considerable distance before bedding down, it was probably the result of being pushed the night before.

Case #7

My nephew, Bret Swiertz, shot a nice buck about an hour before dark during the fourth week of Indiana's archery season. The buck jumped and ran hard, simulating a vital hit. My dad teamed up with Bret at dark and they trailed the deer immediately, expecting to locate a nice buck soon.

The arrow, retrieved after 50 yards, was bent about half way down the shaft and penetration appeared to be eight to 10 inches. The trail was good, showing bright colored blood, and they continued far past where they expected to find it. After 200 yards, with blood beginning to subside, they marked the spot and went back to their vehicles.

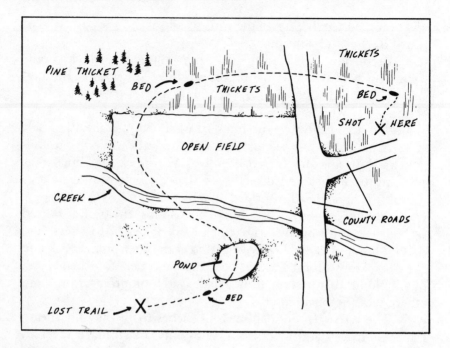

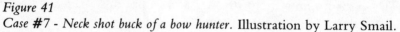

Figure 41
Case #7 - Neck shot buck of a bow hunter. Illustration by Larry Smail.

With a couple of others I joined in to help trail, and it was obvious the buck was not hit through the forward part of the chest, as originally thought. We followed for several hundred more yards, and although the blood remained easy to follow, we were puzzled as to the way the deer moved. Even though it continued westward it seemed to zigzag as it went. It would walk to the left a few feet, then suddenly swing to the right for a few feet. Several times we found where the buck had stood for a long period.

We now suspected that Bret's arrow had hit in front of the shoulders, where the neck joins. We knew we should probably push, since the meat hit was probable, but after several hours were forced to quit until morning. We had covered about 600 to 700 yards, and it was obvious the buck was walking just ahead of us.

Trailing was tougher the next morning because of dried blood, but we stayed on the buck for two hours until we found wet blood just outside a bed. It now seemed as though we had jumped the buck. We continued to trail for about 300 yards across an open field before it finally dropped into a creek, then managed to locate the trail about 50 yards down stream. It had evidently walked through the creek in hopes of losing our trail.

The buck left the creek, entered an area of not so dense thickets, and once again moved in a zigzag pattern, but in about 100 yards we lost the trail. Since it was late afternoon and we were very tired, we decided to call it quits. A couple of guys wanted to hunt for the evening and Bret had lost all hope of recovering the buck, so he looked forward to another evening in the blind.

As everyone prepared to hunt I decided to go back and try to pick up the trail, stay until darkness and give it one last shot.

After a good while of no blood or tracks, I came upon a small pond and in mud on the edge found a set of fresh tracks. I crawled on hands and knees and just before the tracks went into the water, found one drop of blood on a rock. I became fired up, thinking I still had a chance of recovering the buck, since it was obvious it went into the water. I circled the pond and almost directly across found fresh tracks coming out, but no blood. I stayed with the tracks for about 20 yards, picked up a well used deer run and followed it. Within seconds I found a drop of blood, then another, then a blood soaked bed with more blood leaving the bed. I really felt confident. After another hour of slow trailing I managed to follow about 200 more yards, but the blood had slowed to a small drop here and there, then just stopped. With only another hour of daylight left, I looked over a pine thicket ahead. Although the buck had headed directly for it, I found nothing and called it quits at dark.

Total trailing time was 13 hours over $1^1/_2$ miles. From the time the buck was shot until the trail was abandoned, 25 hours elapsed. I am not sure why the buck zigzagged for better than a half mile, but it is possible extreme muscle damage in the neck caused it. I suspect it may also have been done in an attempt to lose its trailers. I feel certain that is why it walked the creek and

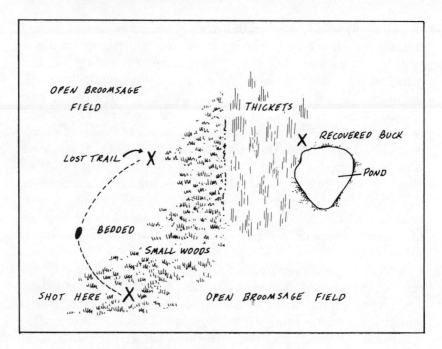

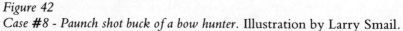

Figure 42
Case #8 - Paunch shot buck of a bow hunter. Illustration by Larry Smail.

crossed through the pond, something it felt it had to do to lose us. Maybe a deer, particularly an older and smarter buck, assumes you are trailing by smell, the same as it does. Naturally, the water could lose us if that were the case.

Case #8

When the small buck stepped into the opening, it was angled slightly towards me at 15 yards. Temptation got the best of me and I took the shot, my arrow entering about midway in the body to angle away from the vitals. I knew it was gut shot and nearly kicked myself out of the tree for not having the patience to wait for a better shot.

The buck turned away with neck drawn closely to its shoulders, walked for 50 yards, then stopped and bedded. It lay on its side, looking around, obviously not knowing what had happened. After an hour the buck came to its feet and slowly walked off. I waited 15 minutes, climbed down, retrieved my arrow and quietly left the woods. I hoped to meet up with the buck later that day.

I returned at about 1 p.m. with my son John. It had been six hours since I shot and I hoped the arrow had done its job. There was a small amount of dried blood where the buck bedded and it took 20 minutes to pick up the trail. I found blood every 10 yards or so, not good for a walking deer, so I knew the exit hole was probably clogged. After another 75 yards, the blood just stopped and I spent an hour searching for more blood that didn't exist, only 125 yards from where the deer was hit. I knew I would have to be lucky to find this buck.

John continued looking for more blood while I walked a few nearby deer runs, but nothing showed up. Now late afternoon, I knew the only chance was to forget looking for blood and try to spot the deer, assuming it was dead.

We spread out about 50 yards apart and combed nearby thickets, hoping it had bedded earlier, but found nothing. Knowing we had to widen our search, I told John to continue checking in a northerly direction, the way the buck had been heading, and I decided to stroll over to a nearby pond. Since I had seen other paunch shot deer recovered by water, I hoped it would happen one more time. As I approached the pond, I made out the shape of a deer lying by the edge of the water and had found the buck.

I was fortunate to recover this buck, which I assumed had bedded beside the water and stayed there until it died. The four pointer had gone 300 yards from where it was shot. Although 10 hours had elapsed, I knew it had been dead for some time, since it was considerably stiff. The arrow had entered the right side, about halfway along the body, and exited just a little lower on the opposite side. The departure hole was plugged with intestinal material, and the entrance hole showed very little blood on the hide. Even when I checked tracks where the buck had approached water, I found no blood. This is a perfect example of why the paunch shot deer should never be pushed.

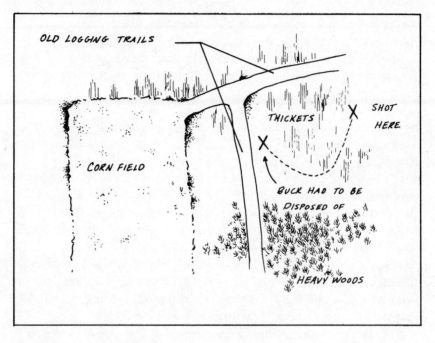

Figure 43
Case #9 - Hip shot buck of a bow hunter. Illustration by Larry Smail.

Case #9

The buck entered the thickets north of me and I heard it walking at least 75 yards away. It ambled down the well-used trail in my direction, but not the one I hoped as the run it was using would pass my stand at 28 yards, not a preferred distance. When the buck began to pass it quartered away, and since the angle couldn't be better I decided to shoot. As the arrow hit I heard a loud "thunk", the buck bolted and ran away at full speed.

I first thought I had made a vital hit, but the loud thunk made me wonder if I had hit the hip. Since unsure, I stayed put until almost dark when I went to where the buck was standing and my arrow was nowhere to be found. I found bright red blood almost immediately and for a moment hoped for the vital hit. I had to meet friends, so marked the spot and headed out, planning to return later.

Since the buck had gone directly toward a logging road I would have to walk, I circled to the southwest and picked up the old road. I hoped to bypass the buck, not disturb it if bedded close by, and walked as quietly as possible. A rustling noise startled me after 200 yards, so I thought I had jumped another deer, but then I saw the buck trying to get up. Its hips were down, front legs up, and I disposed of the buck.

The six pointer was hit through the left hip, the arrow still imbedded and penetration about 12 inches. The buck was not hit through the femoral artery, the only damage was to the hip muscles. The buck had left at a fast running speed, obviously not having difficulty using its legs, but after a 150 yard run went down. This is a perfect example of how damaging the hip shot can be, even when the femoral artery is not severed.

Case #10

My friend Woody Williams and I, drawn for a special hunt at the Crane Naval Depot in southern Indiana, were hunting with shotguns and both hoped for a buck. We had been in the area previously so were familiar with where we should hunt, about a mile apart. Woody planned to walk back at noon to meet me where the vehicle was parked.

I bagged a small spike soon after getting into a tree, so my hunting ended quickly. I later heard a shot from Woody's direction, hoped he had scored, but his face indicated otherwise when he came into view. He said that a decent buck followed a few does and fawns near the tree in which he was perched. He squeezed off a shot, the gun roared, the buck dropped instantly, thrashed violently on the ground trying to get to its feet, but couldn't. Woody could see blood along the deer's back, so assumed it was spine shot. But as he lowered the weapon, the buck got to its feet and ran before he could get off another shot.

We had not had much luck recovering loin hit deer, either by gun or bow, but hoped this time might be different. We picked up the trail, found blood thrown everywhere, and followed easily for about 100 yards to find a bed, but the buck was not in it. The blood trail leaving the bed began to taper off and the buck was going uphill on a slight grade. In about 100 yards it suddenly turned right and started downhill, and soon after we lost the trail. We searched for a couple of hours, but found nothing.

This is a typical loin shot deer trail. After 250 yards the blood just stopped. Many hunters have experienced similar situations, when you think you have spine shot but haven't. When this situation occurs gun hunting, the deer has to be pushed, but even then recovery rates are not good.

Figure 44
Case #10 - *Loin shot buck of a gun hunter.* Illustration by Larry Smail.

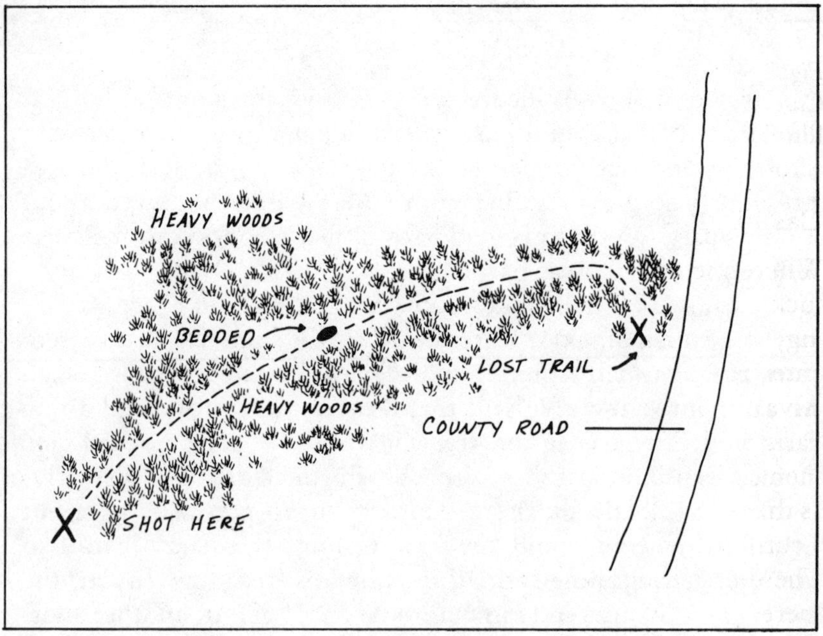

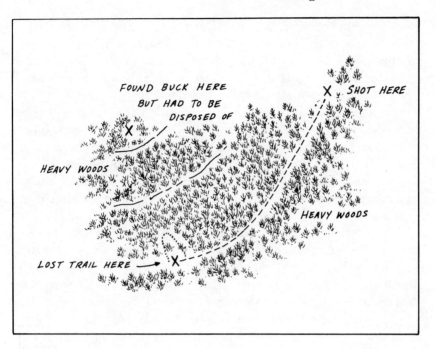

FOUND BUCK HERE
BUT HAD TO BE
DISPOSED OF

X   SHOT HERE

X

HEAVY WOODS

HEAVY WOODS

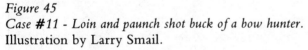
LOST TRAIL HERE ➝ X

Figure 45
Case #11 - Loin and paunch shot buck of a bow hunter.
Illustration by Larry Smail.

Case #11

While bow hunting in Land Between The Lakes, on the Kentucky side, Alva Rinehart arrowed a small buck early one morning, almost straight down from his tree. The arrow appeared to enter the top of the deer's body, just behind the diaphragm. Alva waited for nearly one hour, then found a small amount of dark blood and trailed it for about 50 yards when better judgment told him to stop. A few hours later we followed the trail as the buck walked along the side of a steep ridge, then followed a run for better than 200 yards to the bottom side of the ridge. The blood eventually tapered off and soon stopped. Although there were too many leaves to see tracks, we assumed it was still using the deer trail. With so many leaves, we felt we would have found a drop of blood if the buck was using the run.

We checked where we had lost the blood trail to see if the buck had made an abrupt left turn, and found nothing. I decided to check the steep hill on the other side and spotted leaves that appeared freshly rustled. I had seen whitetails go uphill when hit, but usually not a grade this steep.

I made a little loop about 20 yards up the hill, found a drop of blood, and we all began climbing. We found no blood, only rustled leaves, and it seemed to take forever to get to the peak at least 150 yards uphill. As Alva hit the top he jumped back and said, "There it is!" We rushed up expecting to see a dead buck, but instead saw the buck alive and bedded. Another shot disposed of it.

The four pointer had lain on top of the hill and watched us the whole time, probably too sick to get up. It had been there for about five hours and had gone 400 yards, 150 yards a steep uphill grade. Although there was loin damage, I am sure the destroyed paunch decided its destiny.

Throughout this chapter you have read about the reactions of many types of wounded whitetails. Some acted as expected, some didn't. Either way, past experiences help prepare us for future experiences.

I did not discuss any vitally hit deer cases in this chapter, simply because it was not necessary. The vitally hit deer will die quickly, whether pushed or left alone. I have heard some hunters say they hit a deer right where it counts, through the heart and lungs, but trailed the deer for a long distance and never found it. I say this is "hogwash", it can't happen. If a deer is hit in the boiler room, it's dead and quickly. There are situations where only one lung might be hit, and this may change the end result, but most of the time a hunter has mistaken his hit location.

A hunter should keep records of trailing experiences. There is a lot that none of us can really explain, but the experiences can help us in the future. Many biologists are unsure of certain wound reactions, mainly because there is no humane way of testing, but hunters test it every year. Our results can be the discoveries.

CHAPTER 15

TRAILING THE WOUNDED BLACK BEAR

Many may wonder why I decided to write a chapter on trailing a wounded black bear in a book based on whitetails. The popularity of black bear hunting has increased by a large margin in recent years. More and more advertisements on guided bear hunts are seen in hunting magazines. Many hunters have participated in bear hunts and many others will do so. Even hunters who do not live in black bear areas go after this great challenge. Most have probably hunted deer for several years, then have the urge to seek another prize. The average deer hunter who hits a black bear will react and trail the animal in much the same fashion as he would the whitetail, except with more caution.

For 10 years I have gone to Ontario, Canada, hunting the black bear both in the spring and the fall. I have spent every trip hunting over baits which some feel is unsportsmanlike. But, unless you have tried it you don't realize the great challenge this magnificent animal offers.

I have been hooked since my very first encounter with the black bear, and it is in my blood for life. I have bagged several

175

bears, with bow and gun, although most trips were with the bow. I have participated in many trailing adventures, some my own reconnaissance and some with others. I enjoy it tremendously and look forward to each season.

As is with the whitetail, or any game animal, shot placement is a crucial decision for the black bear hunter. It may be even more important than with any other animal, simply because trailing can be very difficult. Poorly hit black bear recovery rate is not very high.

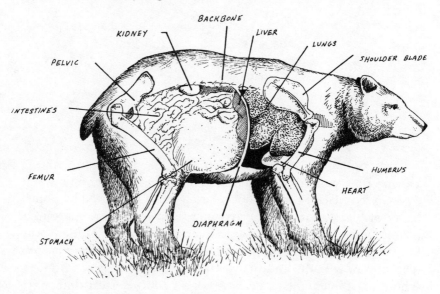

Figure 46
Anatomy of a black bear. Illustration by Larry Smail.

Anyone involved in a black bear hunt should know and understand the anatomy. One important factor is to realize that the black bear's lungs lie much farther forward than the whitetail's. A hit only inches behind the shoulder from a broadside angle may not strike the vital lungs. The broadside shot should not be taken unless you have complete confidence that you can hit the spot you are aiming for. The gun hunter can take a broadside shot and risk hitting the shoulder, providing the firearm has enough caliber to do the job. If it doesn't, he has no business being there. Most of the time gun hunters are over-equipped, pack more power than they need and feel if they are going after bear they should tote a cannon along.

The bow hunter should think twice before taking a broad-side shot. If the arrow hits more than three inches behind the shoulder, he may be in for another hunt to fill his tag. The bow hunter should be very patient before taking a shot. The bear, if given enough time, will usually turn and quarter away, offering easy entrance into the vitals. This is particularly true if hunting over baits.

Patience is usually more of a problem for a gun hunter, who will sometimes shoot as soon as the bear comes into view. Since I began bear hunting with a bow, I learned how to mix patience and bears. During my first trip to Ontario I spent an hour watching a blackie on bait, only 12 yards from the base of my tree. All I had heard since I had arrived was to wait for the perfect shot. The bear never turned to offer a quartering-away shot while on the bait. After it had eaten all the bait, temptation got the best of me and I took a quartering-into shot, big "no-no". The arrow struck the shoulder with only six-inch penetration, so I learned my lesson the hard way. After this I waited to take the best shots, and even when I go hunting with a muzzleloader, I don't shoot until the bear offers a quartering-away shot.

The frontal, or facing-away shot should never be taken by the bow hunter, is not a wise choice for the gun hunter, and is usually made by overly anxious hunters. If a person hunts over bait, the bear will usually become occupied with eating and present a decent shot. A hunter stalking black bear, or hunting with hounds, must react accordingly as the perfect quartering-away shot may never be offered.

I prefer to shoot a bear only slightly quartering away, to allow room for error. A black bear angling away sharply will create as much of a problem as a quartering-into shot. You must aim farther back in order to get into the vitals which presents the risk of hitting the hip.

A bear hunter should not aim too low or too high. Any arrow high in the back will usually be stopped quickly and it is risky to aim too low as hunters are fooled by hair that hangs under the bear. You tend to think there is more bear than there is, particularly crucial when the shot is from a tree stand. I usually like to get no higher than 14 feet, as the shot angle will become a determining factor. You may get a wad of bear hair, nothing more, so I am more prone to shoot a little high because of this. With the arrow on a downward angle, if the hit is just a little under the back it will go down into the vitals.

One recommendation to any bow hunter planning a black bear hunt is to purchase and test a string tracker. As I mentioned in Chapter 12, they do work, and I believe they are invaluable when bow hunting black bear. Unless you are hunting in late spring or early summer, when the hide is nearly rubbed out, you will find the thick hide of the black bear soaks up blood from the wound before it gets to the ground. This makes trailing very difficult as only a small amount of blood finds its way to the ground in many cases. Even if the hit is in the vital area, it is possible blood will be sparse, and not comparable to the same hit in a whitetail.

Figure 47
The broadside shot should only be taken if the hunter has complete confidence that he can hit his spot. Illustration by Larry Smail.

The string tracker can make a major difference in black bear trailing. Many times blood is not found on a poorly hit bear until the animal has gone 100 or more yards. Not only does this make recovery difficult, it is tough to get started. A string tracker puts you on the trail immediately.

I find the heavier pound test line will do the best job. Black bears are tough critters and sometimes, if poorly hit, just seem to go and go to the thickest cover they can. I presume this is because they spend most of their lives in this type of territory. Even the heavier pound test line can break, but if you have trailed a wounded bruin for 200 yards when it does break, you can begin trailing at that point. Lets face it, you're 200 yards closer than you might have been without the tracker, and it is possible the bear may have gone only a short distance farther.

Probably nothing can beat the use of good hounds when trailing a wounded bear, especially one that is leaving no blood. I have never been fortunate enough to have the aid of hounds, but if you are lucky enough to gain their use you are a big step ahead. A good hound trails the bruin by scent, not by the amount of blood on the ground. Even if you must leave a bear for several hours to obtain hounds, a good dog will still pick up the trail, unless there is a hard rain.

The vital lungs and heart of the average black bear are a fraction smaller than those of an adult whitetail, but are just as vital and must be considered as the target to aim for. The lung shot will put a large bruin down quickly. When bow hunting, all of my lung shot bears have gone down in less than 50 yards. One that I took with a .50 caliber Hawkins muzzleloader managed to go about 70 yards, as far as I have seen any blackie go when hit through both lungs. Tom Hodges, who has accompanied me on several Ontario bear hunts, put a bruin down in only 12 yards after a perfect arrow shot. The black bear seems to succumb sooner than the whitetail hit through the lungs, in my experience.

Several bears that I have arrow shot through the vitals have shown a tendency to turn and snap at the side the arrow hits. They snap their jaws and let out a "barf", then go into a hard, dead run, belly low to the ground. I have seen them fall, get up and run a few short yards, fall again and even get back up again in only a few seconds. The vitally hit bruin covers ground quickly and I do not want to stand in a direct line with an oncoming wounded bear.

The blood of the lung and heart shot bruin will be bright red, as with the whitetail. If the exit is low, near one of the front legs, the trail can usually be found quite easily. If the exit is high, a lot less blood will get to the ground, most of it being absorbed by the thick hide.

I am not usually fortunate enough to find frothy blood, as with the lung shot whitetail. One reason may be because the bear generally doesn't travel as far. Also, a recovered lung shot bear often has many air bubbles on the blood-saturated hide, but it usually doesn't get to the ground.

. Quite often the hunter sees a vitally hit bear go down, but this is unusual for me. Most areas I hunt in are extremely thick and visibility is poor. Usually my bait is only 10 to 15 yards from the tree I am perched in, whether with gun or bow, and visibility past the bait may be only 20 yards or less. Since I may not see the bear go down, I pay close attention to departing bear sounds. As long as I can hear it running, I get an idea of how far it has gone, and many times I hear it fall. Wounded bears will often run over everything in their path, including large log jams, and make quite a racket leaving an area. I pay close attention to particular landmarks the bear might run past, very important when little blood may be found. And, you can't believe how quietly a wounded bear can run, even at full speed, in some areas near swamps and quite mossy. Paunch shot or liver shot bears are the toughest to trail, and my recovery rate is very poor compared to whitetails shot in those locations. Trailing is difficult and if you ever needed a hound, this is the time.

It is best to wait several hours before taking up the trail of a paunch or liver shot black bear, and I prefer to wait overnight if it was shot in the late afternoon. This animal should not be pushed under any circumstances, and I will not trail a paunch shot bear even if rain is forecast. I may consider taking up the trail if I am sure the shot has severed the liver, but this is hard to determine as a bow shot, and impossible from a gun shot. If my arrow entered just behind the diaphragm, and is coated with dark red blood, I assume I have hit the liver. I then take up the trail if rain is about to begin.

Figure 48
The quartering away shot offers you the best chance for the quickest kill.
Illustration by Larry Smail.

The dark red trail is not picked up quickly, and in some instances I have gone 100 yards before blood was found. Blood drops will usually be spaced, sometimes several yards apart, so trailing must be done slowly. This is one time to pay close attention to brush and high weeds for rubbed off blood, perhaps the only way to trail the bear. After it has gone a distance, the hide will become saturated and begin rubbing blood off as it passes through or over obstacles.

The liver hit black bear leaves a better blood trail than the paunch shot bruin, but the trail is not significantly different as trailing will be difficult either way. The paunch shot may clog the exit hole and even less blood will get to the ground.

I prefer to trail this bear with at least one other person, preferably two. It is nice to have one watching ahead for the bear in case another shot is needed.

Unlike the whitetail, it is less likely for the liver or paunch shot bruin to bed down. They seem to keep going, even though not pushed, and I am not sure why. Don't expect the paunch shot or liver shot bear to bed down after a couple of hundred yards, although they do in a few rare circumstances. They are often not trailed even that far because the trail is lost and after only a short distance the hunter is forced to give up.

If extremely fortunate, you may recover the liver or paunch shot bear without the aid of hounds or string trackers. One thing is certain, after this kind of hit your work will be cut out for you. This is a good reason to realize how important it is to wait for the quartering-away shot.

Major arteries are much the same as in the whitetail, and will put a bruin down quickly when severed. One good friend took a nice blackie by severing the aortic artery. The arrow had hit high in the back, missing the vital lungs by inches. What could have been a half day trailing job ended up in 10 minutes. You are usually just plain lucky to hit a bear in one of its major arteries.

The meat hit can be discouraging for the bear hunter. I have had no luck attempting to recover a bear hit in the muscle areas only as they seem to keep going and going. I did get my hopes up on one Ontario blackie that was not well hit a few years ago. The bear had approached the bait after attempting to do so for better than an hour. It had circled me, gone to my right, my left, but it seemed it would never walk that final few steps into bow range. After finally going to the bait, it turned perfectly quartering-away, so I drew and aimed on the seemingly easy target. The arrow struck high and much too far back, penetration only a few inches, so I knew I was in trouble. I waited a short time and then left the area as quietly as possible.

The next morning a friend and I found the blood trail within 40 yards of the shot. Blood was not in great abundance, but was steady enough to follow easily, which impressed me since the bear was running at full speed. We trailed across a small creek where it started up a fairly steep hill, went straight up for about 100 yards and we found a bed with dried blood in it. It was obvious the bruin had been gone for several hours. We trailed for another 50 yards, found another bed with dried blood, but could find no more and the trail was lost. We did find the feathered half of my arrow about 20 yards from the last bed, but it didn't help. We searched the surrounding area for a couple of hours in hopes of spotting the bear down somewhere, but nothing turned up. I also managed to lose the best hunting knife I ever owned, a sad day overall.

It had been unusual to find beds so close to where the bruin was shot. I hoped there was enough damage done by the arrow, but there obviously wasn't. I hated to lose the old boy, a big one, the largest black bear I ever shot at with a bow.

The hip shot, when the femoral artery is missed, does not seem to be as damaging to a bear as to a whitetail. As you read in previous chapters, severe hip muscle damage can put a whitetail down, but this is not the case with the black bear. I am not sure if it is tougher through the hips or for other reasons, but I have not been involved in enough hip shot bears to be a fair judge.

Sometimes it is possible to trail the black bear without finding blood, by tracks alone. The feet are flat and well padded and it is possible for the animal to leave sign as it passes through an area, even though not crossing a soft surface. In mossy areas, the bear will leave an obvious pad print, the heavier the bear the better chance of finding tracks.

The average width of the front feet of an adult black bear is about 3½ to 4 inches, the hind feet about 6 to 6½ inches in length. Bears in the 400 pound class or larger will naturally have larger feet. The front pads will be wide with no depth, whereas the hind feet will be long with less width. Hind claws are much shorter than those on the front feet.

Claw marks, usually not noticeable in tracks unless the bear walks through mud or sand, will appear directly in front of the toes.

When trailing by tracks alone, some hunters tend to think the front foot is the long print and the short pad is the hind foot, but it is just the opposite. The bear places its hind foot in front of its front feet as it walks.

Hunters think trailing a wounded black bear is dangerous, and therefore they should pack some heavy artillery. I don't believe trailing a wounded blackie puts your life in jeopardy, but common sense must be used. Although it is unlikely a black bear will attack a trailer, it is capable of doing so. Fortunately, a common fear of man will usually deter this move.

I have packed a gun on occasion just in case, usually when trailing a poorly hit bear that is apt to have some life left when I catch up. I have never had to use it, although a couple of times I wondered if I might.

If you face a situation where you feel a gun is necessary, by all means take it along if the law permits. The gun I have found best is my 12 gauge Ithaca Deerslayer, loaded with slugs. It has a short barrel that makes it easy to swing quickly, and is ideal for dense cover, which is where a lot of wounded blackies may lead you. It has open sights, allowing quick aim, and the slug has a lot of knockdown power to handle the job.

I have seen some hunters take up the trail of a wounded blackie while lugging a big rifle with a scope on it. Since they hunt with it, they feel it is the right choice. This is better than no gun, but the short-barrelled slug gun should be packed along if there is a chance of an encounter. More likely you will meet a bear at close yardage.

It is important to mark your trail well, especially in unfamiliar territory. Toilet paper, or the line of a string tracker, will serve the purpose. Be sure to gather up spent line after trailing.

A lost blood trail does not mean the bear will not die, so the hunter should continue to look as long as possible. Internal bleeding may determine how soon the bear will go down, provided a major artery is not severed.

Quiet trailing is a must. The hunter should not try to keep the animal moving as the farther you must trail the better chance of losing it. If the bear is jumped up, take another shot and put it down if possible.

I don't prefer night trailing, but I have had to do it on occasion, usually being forced by weather. I crawled on hands and knees through an alder thicket where visibility was only 10 feet during the daylight, so imagine how it was in the dark. I realize when I look back I had to be some kind of a nut. Most of the time I trail a bear in the dark only if I am sure it was a good hit, if I saw the bear go down, or found a lot of frothy blood indicating a good lung hit.

It is wise to keep all participating hunters fairly close together if night trailing. The last thing you want is some guy to shoot at a noise in the dark, so be sure everyone knows where each person is at all times. Although an individual may not be trigger-happy, a lot of things change when on the trail of an animal capable of killing.

I shot a decent blackie one evening just before dark. I found my arrow only a few feet beyond where the bear had been standing. The arrow looked as though it had only scraped the

Figure 49
The walking black bear will leave hind foot prints in front of front feet. Claw marks are only visible on an extremely soft surface.
Illustration by Larry Smail.

under side of the bear, but since the shot was up front there was an outside chance it had penetrated enough to slice the heart.

With rain threatening, I took up the trail that night and three others participated. One insisted on his .30-.06, saying he felt a lot safer with it.

Woody Williams with a nice Ontario blackie.

The bear led us into an area of thick brush, so we had to go slowly and bend over just to squeeze through. While in the middle of the thick stuff, one guy heard a noise. I heard nothing, but this put me on edge. After trailing a few more yards, the guy once again heard something and was sure it was just up ahead. Now we were all becoming quite nervous. I got the gut feeling we should call the whole thing off and back our way out, but we knew we would surely get out at any time and decided to keep going. Someone hollered, "What was that?" Everyone stopped, I turned slowly, and the guy behind had his rifle pointed at my head, shining a flashlight over me. I had the feeling his finger was on the trigger and kindly asked him to turn the weapon away.

This is a perfect example of how some hunters, particularly beginning bear hunters, can react. I understand we should take the bear seriously, but I think I was in more danger of being accidentally shot that night than being attacked by an angry bear. We stopped trailing soon after, returned the next morning, but found nothing.

There are methods to deter an attack if you are worried about trailing wounded bears. You can clang pots and pans together as you walk, or you can talk in a loud voice. I have heard some people carry an umbrella when in an area where bears are present. I guess it can be opened to guard off a bear if it is close. I suppose a spray can of mace might help during a close encounter, but I prefer not to get that close. An unarmed hunter would be wise to get up a tree as fast as possible.

If you trail a bear in the dark be sure to have good flashlights or use a couple of gas powered lanterns. Even then, not much will show in thick woods.

A friend was certain he made a good hit on a large sow one evening, so we took up the trail that night. The blood in 50 yards led us to an area of downed timber. We had no choice but to go over each pile, as the bear had done. In the lead I stepped over a log and tripped on something soft and hairy. Fortunately the sow was quite dead.

A hunter will often hear a death bawl if the bear goes down close to your position. I have heard it all but twice on lung shot bear. Many experts claim a gun shot black bear is more apt to let out a bawl, but every bear I have taken with a bow did so.

The moan, or bawl, is unmistakable. You will know what it is when you hear it. It starts out low in volume and increases, and some bears do this several times, others only once or twice. Younger bears usually let out a longer, louder moan than older bruins, and I am not sure why.

It is also possible to hear a cough or two with a good lung hit. I heard one bear run about 50 yards and pile up with all quiet and no bawl. I did hear it cough twice, not at all loud. Since there were no moans, I wondered if I hit the bear effectively. The next morning I found it right where it had coughed, hit through both lungs.

Some bear hunters, particularly beginners, are often afraid to climb out of a tree stand after they have watched a bear go down. One fellow shot a bear 30 yards from his stand, and even though he had shot with a rifle, decided to shoot again and again, just to be on the safe side. The bear had stopped moving seconds after the first shot, but he wasn't going to take a chance. It was his first evening on a bait and he had never seen a bear in the wild. We had just put the guy up a tree and walked off when the bear came in. A lot of guys might have missed the first shot simply because of nervousness.

If a bear goes down where you can see it, watch for any movement. If you did not hear a death moan, there is a chance the bear is still alive. By staying put, you will gain reassurance after a while that the bear is indeed dead.

My most frightening experience came during a second trip to Ontario. I baited just inside a pine thicket about 300 yards across an open pasture and a bear came about an hour before dark. There was a slight hill behind, allowing the bear to get even with me, and as a breeze was blowing directly toward it, it caught my scent only 50 yards away, and after a couple of "woofs" it took off. This didn't bother me much since bears had done this before. It tried to come in two more times, but each time stopped and repeated the procedure.

Time passed and I saw nothing more of the bear. It got darker and darker, and as I was about to lower my bow a stick cracked up the hill. I thought, "Darn, it's back." Minutes passed, but there was no woofing. Was it on the hill or close by? The breeze had died and all was calm, so once again I attempted to lower my bow when I heard the bear about 15 yards from my stand. It walked up to only five yards from the base of my tree and stopped. I could barely see its outline in the dark.

Then the real trouble started. The bear popped its jaws and paced back and forth, head turned upward, and I felt it was looking right at me. After a couple of minutes this bear had begun to really shake me up. I knew it was going to start up the tree, and the longer it popped its jaws, the angrier it seemed to get.

I knew I had to do something as it was getting very dark. Since I was using a lighted sight pin, I decided to shoot at the bear in the dark, knowing I would have to be really lucky. I heard a loud "thunk" when I released and knew I hit the bear, which turned and ran. I was glad it was gone, but it ran directly into the pasture I had to cross to get out. I scratched my head for a while, pondering what to do, knowing I could not wait for anybody to come and get me. The vehicle was on the road and I was supposed to pick up my buddies, hunting about 10 miles from me. I was already late and it was pitch black.

I quietly got out of the tree, grabbed my flashlight and my bow, and walked to the pasture with my light off. I thought of taking off on a dead run across 300 yards of pasture, but figured I couldn't make it. The light only illuminated in close proximity, so I nocked an arrow, loosened my knife from its sheath and was ready.

I continued to shine the light in circles as I walked out in the pasture. After what seemed like an eternity I reached the road, jumped in the truck and locked the door. I realize now how foolish I must have looked.

The next morning we followed a few drops of blood into the pasture, where I found my bent arrow with blood only four inches up the shaft. It was obviously a shoulder hit. We trailed the bear directly through the pasture, the same way I had gone, but lost the blood after about 150 yards. I never knew where the bear went, but I was certainly glad I had not met up with it the previous night. Had I hollered that night, it probably would have left and I would not have had to risk taking a shot. It was frightening, but I might react in much the same manner in the same situation. I know it is poor judgment to take a shot under those conditions, but it seemed the only way to get the bear out of there.

When you see your bear lying up ahead, approach only from the rear, never walk in front until you are sure it is dead. Usually I take my bow or gun barrel and give a few good pokes. Pay close attention to the eyes and whether or not it is still breathing.

Sometimes when I approach a downed bear I will be able to see where the arrow or bullet hole is. I still poke a time or two, but the hole will give you a good indication of the damage. If the hole is somewhere other than in a vital area, be very certain the bear is dead before approaching. Use a long stick if one is handy. If there is any sign of life, don't hesitate to shoot again. It is far easier for a taxidermist to patch up another hole than it is for a doctor to patch you up.

As I stressed at the beginning of this chapter, it is so important to take only a shot that will give you quick kill. The wounded black bear is one of the most difficult big game animals to recover, if poorly hit. All this can be bypassed if you have the patience to wait it out. It will sooner or later offer you the shot you have practiced and waited for.

CHAPTER 16

RECOVERY OF THE WHITETAIL

I have always believed that many whitetails are recovered because the hunter didn't give up. On the other hand, a lot of wounded whitetails die and rot away because a deer hunter gave up too soon.

Since the blood trail has stopped or has been lost, some hunters think they should give it up. They may spend several hours trailing, but when sign ceases, they call it quits. There are times this is valid, but often it isn't. If a hunter is sure, beyond any reasonable doubt, that the wound was only superficial, then the trail should be abandoned. The whitetail will recover and the hunter can return to hunting.

A bow hunter is often given the opportunity to see where the arrow hit, or to find his spent arrow. This may provide enough evidence to know the wound was insignificant. He trails the deer as far as possible, but after a long distance gains more confidence that the hit was not lethal.

The gun hunter rarely knows for sure where his bullet hit, and can only judge by the deer's reaction and the type of blood trail. However, there can still be a lot of doubt when he decides to stop trailing.

I firmly believe that any deer hit through the body cavity will most likely die, whether shot by an arrow or bullet. I am including any wound to the animal from behind the shoulders to just in front of the hips. A wound in this area will do some type of organ damage and cause internal bleeding. When I trail a deer I am sure was hit in this portion of the body, I continue to trail it. When the blood stops and there is no more sign to follow, I continue to look. I might quit for a few hours, or I might stop overnight, but I usually go back, not with the intention of finding new blood, but of locating the deer.

Some people urge me to give up knowing I will never find the deer, but if I continue looking I feel better when I do decide to abandon the search. At least I know I gave it all I could.

Maybe one reason I have always hated to give up on a whitetail that I assume will die is because I lost the first deer I killed. It wasn't found until three days after it was shot. During my beginning days of bow hunting, young and inexperienced, a doe passed my stand about 60 yards away, and since the angle was good I decided to shoot. I would not attempt a ridiculous shot like that now, but as with most youngsters, I wanted to kill my first deer. About the time the arrow got to the doe I heard a loud "thunk" and knew I had hit either a tree or the deer. It was late evening so I decided to get out of my tree and return later with others.

I was greeted by one of my friends when I got back to my dad's vehicle extremely excited as he had just hit a small buck. A short time later we all joined to trail his deer, found the buck quickly, and he was one proud hunter.

I explained that I didn't know if I had hit a doe or missed, so everyone volunteered to look that night if I wanted. Not having much confidence in my shooting ability, I said I would look by myself in the morning. Since I was inexperienced at trailing, I would need help if I had hit the deer, but I knew I would be embarrassed to find my arrow sticking in a tree.

The next morning I began checking trees en route to where the deer was standing when I had shot. I was surprised not to find the arrow, and when I found blood I whooped and hollered, figuring I would soon tag my first deer. I pulled my-self together and began the scary job of trailing the deer alone. Blood was easy to follow for 100 yards and I felt confident, then the blood trail began to diminish and I lost it completely in another 100 yards. I spent the rest of the day just looking for the doe, and was discouraged to find nothing.

Three days later I returned for a morning hunt from the same stand. An old coon hound followed me and I couldn't get rid of it. The dog was content to lie at the base of an oak tree only 20 yards from my stand, stayed there until I climbed down, and I knew it was useless to count on a deer showing up with the hound right there. I figured to follow the doe's trail in hopes of finding my arrow, realizing there was a chance I might have missed it, and that it could tell me a lot.

I followed the trail to where I had lost it but found no arrow, the dog still tagging along. It flushed a covey of quail, seemed to enjoy the walk, and in a dense area of honeysuckle the hound's tail wagged in excitement. I expected a rabbit to pop out, but the dog stayed in one place. I walked into the honey-suckle and there was my doe. I rolled the deer over, found my arrow in the deer's right side, and realized it had been a liver hit. The deer had gone only 250 yards.

Although I had checked the honeysuckle over, it was evi-dent I had blown it. Obviously I didn't check well enough, and I am sure I probably walked right by the doe while combing the honeysuckle. A wounded whitetail will often go into thick cover, particularly if it wants to bed down or knows it is being pushed. It will sometimes pick out the thickest terrain in an attempt to completely conceal itself. If there is no blood trail to lead the hunter, it requires a lot of time and patience to find the deer. In these cases I prefer several other hunters to help out. As stated earlier, I prefer only one or two besides myself when following a blood trail, but otherwise the more eyes looking the better. The trailing is over and the only chance of finding the deer is to actually see it. Several people can cover an area more easily and quickly than one or two and increase recovery chances.

It is important in dense cover to check the area as thoroughly as possible for any thick spot where the deer could be lying. A deer has a way of blending in with laurel, briars, honeysuckle, almost any type of thick cover. Many times when I hunt rabbits during January, I walk through thick stuff and come across a decomposing deer that was probably lost by a hunter. Many times this happens because the hunter did not fulfill a responsibility to do everything he could to recover the deer.

In Chapter 14, Case 1, I told of a paunch shot buck that was recovered the following day, 30 hours after it had been shot. The bow hunter who shot was the one who finally spotted the downed buck in an area of honeysuckle, a 40 acre plot of thickets and entanglements. This hunter felt certain the buck was somewhere in the plot, and was not going to quit until he had checked every thicket in there. It paid off.

An area that spells trouble is high grass, or broom sage fields. When a whitetail goes down in waist-high grass, it is almost impossible to see unless you step on it.

One year hunting the Land Between The Lakes in Kentucky, a companion gut shot a doe. He watched the deer go for a good ways when it finally entered a high broom sage field. The field was about five acres and he could see all around it, never saw the deer come out, so we assumed it was down in the high grass. As expected, we trailed only a short way in when we lost the blood. We spent the entire afternoon going through the field but never found it. I still feel certain the deer was in there somewhere.

When looking for a downed deer it is a good practice to concentrate on something white, rather than on the whole deer. If the deer is in thick cover it is unlikely that you are going to see the complete deer, which might be the case if it is lying in an open woods or field.

I recovered one liver shot buck only because I saw the white belly. I shot the deer the evening before and trailed about 300 yards. After losing the blood trail, I concentrated on finding the deer. I walked until I was about blue in the face, made one last excursion along a creek that would lead back to the road and noticed something white about 40 yards on the other side. I thought it was an old bucket, but the more I looked the more I wondered. Since the creek was deep, I almost talked myself out of crossing, but am glad I didn't. It was my buck and I felt great about finding it, especially since I had already found one buck that day that wasn't mine. Imagine spending hours looking, spotting a deer ahead, only to realize it isn't even yours? Earlier that morning I found a buck already dead for a couple of days, that had a larger rack than the one I shot. I certainly felt good when I spotted another white belly later.

Bucks, especially those with large antlers, are sometimes located because the hunter sees the antlers and nothing else. It's always a good feeling to see a shining antler up ahead when you are looking for a buck. The antlers have a tendency to show up easily, especially if the sun is on them. I have often noticed a downed buck's antler before I see the deer. It helps if the buck you are looking for had nicely polished horns before you shot. A drabby brown antler will not be easily seen, but if the tips of the points are white it helps.

Other white portions of the deer can be noticed as well, such as the inside of the ears, the white throat patch, or the white rump. It pays to look for anything white, so if you see something white up ahead, by all means check it out. A few extra steps could mean the difference between filling a tag or going back to hunting.

When I trail a whitetail alone and end up losing the blood trail, I find that using a zigzag method sometimes pays off in locating the downed deer. I usually begin at the point where the blood trail stopped, walk to my right for a distance of about 75 yards, make a sharp cut back to my left and go about 100 yards in that direction. I continue to cut back and forth and increase my distance in one particular direction each time I cut right or left.

The zigzag pattern's direction is the direction the deer was going when the trail was lost. By increasing distance each time I change direction, I might even find the deer if it had turned. It is just a matter of being able to see the deer, and hopefully I will pass close enough so it won't be missed. If others help, the area can be covered more efficiently by spreading a short distance apart and walking a given direction for a certain distance. The zigzag pattern merely enables me to cover the surrounding area as well as one person can.

If I am not able to come up with anything with the zigzag pattern, I resort to checking nearby deer runs. If the deer was using a trail when the blood was lost, I walk this trail for at least another 200 yards. I also check any trails that might intercept into the trail the deer was using, and I walk them for a considerable distance.

If the deer was not on a trail when the blood was lost, I find any trails close by and walk each, going in the general direction the deer was going. I also locate any creeks up ahead and walk the banks in both directions. You may find fresh tracks going up the other side, and if you do, it would be wise to follow them. They could lead to a dead deer.

Sometimes you locate the deer by walking the creek bank. I know of two occasions when we have found deer lying just beside the bank, and in both situations the creek banks were fairly steep. I am not sure if the deer didn't want to attempt to go up, or if they felt safer being down in between the banks. They might have stayed put simply because they felt somewhat hidden.

If you have done everything you can, but still feel your deer is down, try to locate a topographic map of the area. I have found it best to mark on your map the location where the deer was shot, then draw a line across the map in the direction the deer went. Mark it again where you lost the trail and plan a search from there. Mark off all areas that you have already searched thoroughly and concentrate on other areas of possibility.

The topo map will show open fields, heavily timbered areas, fence lines, power lines, drainages, ponds, the complete landscape if it is not too outdated. I would look in open pastures or fields only as a last resort. I would concentrate efforts in the areas of thickets, pine woods, or heavy timber, the areas wounded whitetail generally go to.

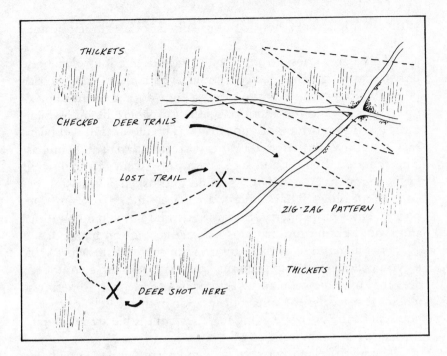

THICKETS

CHECKED   DEER TRAILS

LOST TRAIL   X

ZIG-ZAG PATTERN

THICKETS

X   DEER SHOT HERE

Figure 50
The zigzag pattern used by the author when trailing alone.
Illustration by Larry Smail.

The topo map will also show the land contour with eleva-
tions marked on a scale that shows increasing grid lines. This
helps locate a nearby ridge where a deer might head for. It also
shows bottomland areas that surround the ridges. I have seen
bucks claim a ridge as home territory, and have always felt that
wounded bucks, mainly older ones, go back to areas where they
have spent most of their time. I don't mean the areas covered
while in rut, but early fall areas where they spent days bedded in
a safe and sound place.

Most wounded deer I have trailed usually begin to circle
within one quarter of a mile or less. In some cases it might be
one half a mile, although many times a big buck seems to go in
one direction or circle only slightly. I believe these bucks are

in rut, shot in an area they do not usually use and off their beaten path.

There are times a hunter will trail a deer a long distance, only to have it go onto posted ground, which places one in a bad position. He doesn't want to trespass, nor does he want to give up. A hunter told me about one situation where he hit a small buck the first morning of gun season. The blood trail had been easy to follow, but after 200 yards it crossed a road and entered a posted area. Being good sportsmen, they went to the nearby farmer who had posted the ground and asked permission to continue trailing. The farmer wasted no time in refusing the right to enter his property, explained that he allowed no hunting and would phone authorities if he caught them on his land.

Fortunately not all land owners are this selfish. Most will let you proceed if you explain that you are following a wounded deer that may die soon and was shot in a legal area. Sometimes it helps if you offer to leave your weapon in the vehicle, or to say you will be the only one going in. If several people are involved, the landowner may refuse.

I believe if a landowner refuses you permission to enter he is acting very selfishly. I understand someone not allowing you to hunt, but cannot understand refusing you to go after a wounded deer that may waste away if not recovered. A hunter might suggest the landowner follow the trail, and maybe he would attempt to locate it for you.

Many hunters must wonder how many wounded deer are retrieved. Is the unretrieved rate considerably higher than the recovery rate? There have been studies on recovery rates for both bow and gun hunters, and I will show you records I have kept since my deer hunting first began.

Trailing the wounded deer has always excited and interested me. Since my first trailing experience, I have kept records of types of hits, distances the wounded deer traveled, and how often they were recovered. These records are very helpful for future trailing experiences.

I listed every part of the whitetail's body that could have been wounded. In some cases only predictions could be made, simply because there was no proof of the hit location. I have included both arrow and gun wounds. These appear in a table on the following page.

Of the 15 lung and heart shot deer not recovered, most were due to shoulder hits by arrows, with very little penetration. I feel certain these deer recovered from their wounds.

The liver and paunch wounded deer were recovered about two-thirds of the time, a high percentage. The average distance trailed of any unretrieved paunch shot deer was 800 yards, due in part to a small number that traveled a half mile or more. Many paunch shot deer were trailed 400 yards or less.

The really interesting recovery percentage is the hip shot deer, 13 recovered even though only 6 of these had severed femoral arteries. This shows how damaging the hip shot can be. I can only speculate how many of the eight unretrieved hip shot deer might have died, but my guess is very few. Most were not heavily penetrating shots, speaking of course about arrow wounds. Since these deer were trailed much farther, it would appear that muscle damage was less.

The records show the loin shot deer is tough to recover. This statistic is even less impressive when you take into consideration that all five of the recovered deer were hits that severed the aortic artery, that none were hit through the loin area only.

The neck shot deer was much like the loin shot deer. Two of the three were recovered because of severed carotid arteries, the other because of a severed windpipe. Since I now practice pushing the meat hit deer, something I didn't do years ago when some statistics were compiled, I believe the recovery rate will begin to show a slight increase as time goes on.

The head shot deer that was taken suffered some type of brain damage, as discussed earlier in the book. The other head shots were no more than superficial wounds and I am sure the two deer recovered.

Only one deer taken was hit through the brisket, this by a bow hunter who had a considerable amount of tallow on his arrow. The arrow sliced the underside of the chest and the bottom side of the heart. All other brisket hits were trailed an

Probable Hit Location	Total Trailing Experiences	Total Recoveries	Average Distance Trailed of Recovered Deer	Average Distance Trailed of Unretrieved Deer	Percentage of Recoveries
Lung & Heart	136	121	90 Yards	175 Yards	89%
Liver	30	18	275 Yards	350 Yards	60%
Paunch	57	39	400 Yards	800 Yards	68%
Hips	21	13	200 Yards	325 Yards	62%
Loin	31	5	90 Yards	200 Yards	16%
Neck	7	3	80 Yards	225 Yards	42%
Head	3	1	20 Yards	150 Yards	33%
Brisket Tallow Present	5	1	100 Yards	150 Yards	20%
Unkown	18	0	0	225 Yards	0%
Total	308	202			66%

average of only 150 yards, the wounds not severe enough to have caused death.

Of course none of the 18 unknown locations were recovered or we would have known where the deer had been hit. Most were gun wounds that left us puzzled as to the hit location. Many times I would be fairly certain of a hit and place it into the probable category, but I am sure there were times these judgments were wrong. Overall, I feel the records are very close to the hit locations.

I believe the records will emphasize the fact that a hunter should aim only for the vital area. Although the recovery rate of liver and paunch shot deer is good, it is not that impressive when compared to the 88 percent recovery rate of the heart and lung shot deer. I also believe the recovery rates overall are very good, but that this is due to a lot of experience involved. I am not just speaking of myself, but about several others I have trailed with over the years. They are very good at this and I am sure it has been a big factor. Hunting groups that have not had a lot of trailing experience would most likely have a lower recovery rate.

A profile survey was conducted in 1981 of a large portion of resident South Dakota bow hunters. Information gathered included equipment used, amount of time spent bow hunting, wounding success, and attitudes. Results were reported in a bulletin published by the Wildlife Society, and I received permission to reprint. Although the complete report is not published here, the most interesting results are:

Wildlife Society Bulletin 13: 395-398, 1985 copyright Nonreporting, Success, And Wounding By South Dakota Deer Bowhunters - 1981 Kelly B. McPhillips, Raymond L. Linder, and W. Alan Wentz

Knowledge of wounding incidence is important in managing wildlife resources. Haberland and McCaffery (unpubl. rep., Wis. Dep. Nat. Resour., 1976) and Losch and Samuel (1976) deduced that up to 20% of United States bowhunters hit, but did not retrieve (HBNR), a deer during a season. Langenau and Aho

(1983) reported that rate of wounding (percentage of bowhunters reporting deer HBNR) on Houghton Lake Wildlife Research Area, Michigan, was 12%; Gladfelter (1982) reported the rate of wounding by Iowa bowhunters in 1981 was 17%. Incidence of deer wounding by South Dakota bowhunters has not been measured.

Our objectives were to test alternative bowhunter reporting systems, determine ways to improve estimates of reported wounding of deer by bowhunters.

"Unretrieved Deer"

Rate of Wounding. — Bowhunters reported a total of 220 deer HBNR. One hundred seventy-five of 840 bowhunters (21%) reported at least 1 deer HBNR. One bowhunter reported 5 deer HBNR and 83% reported only 1. Croft (1963) reported a range of 1-4 deer HBNR by individual bowhunters in Georgia.

Relationship of Deer HBNR to Deer Harvested. — Wounding rate (total deer HBNR/total deer harvested + total deer HBNR) by bowhunters was 48% or 0.92 deer HBNR/deer harvested. On the U.S. Naval Ammunition Depot, Crane, Indiana, wounding rate was 58% (Stormer et al. 1979), and Croft (1963) reported a wounding rate of 44% in Georgia. We found that 1.7 deer were reported HBNR/100 hunter-days, and 1 deer HBNR/ 15 shots taken in South Dakota. Stormer et al. (1979) reported 6 HBNR deer/100 hunter-days and 1.4 HBNR deer harvested on the U.S. Naval Ammuntion Depot, Crane, Indiana. Michigan bowhunters at the Houghton Lake Wildlife Research Area reported 1.2 deer HBNR for each deer harvested (Langenau and Aho 1983).

Relationship Between Success and Wounding. — Successful bowhunters in the profile survey reported more deer HBNR than unsuccessful bowhunters. Findings from the U.S. Naval Ammunition Depot, Crane, Indiana, were similar (Stormer et al. 1979). Gladfelter et al. (1983) found that unsuccessful Iowa bowhunters were 1.37 times more likely to wound a deer than successful bowhunters, and that consistent rates of wounding, regardless of number of years of experience, suggested that training or field experience would not affect rates of wounding. Croft (1963) found that success increased with years of experience but did not comment on the effect of experience on wounding.

Wounding of deer by bowhunters is occurring at a rate of approximately 1 deer for each deer harvested. Twenty-one percent of all bowhunters sampled reported HBNR by resident bowhunters in 1981 resulted in fatality and were added to the reported bowhunter harvest, the resident harvest for the 1981 archery deer season would be 4,236 deer. This number is only 15% of the 1981 deer harvest in South Dakota and does not appear to be a significant biological factor in deer herd management. However, more information is needed regarding factors affecting wounding by bowhunters and the portion of HBNR deer that die if wildlife managers are going to incorporate this factors into management and harvest plans.

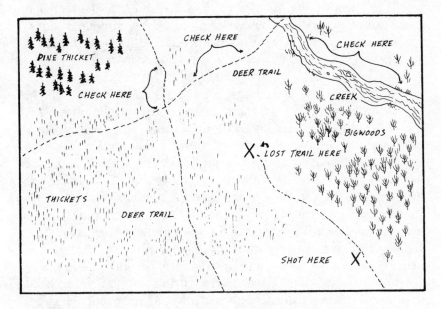

Figure 51
It pays to walk all deer trails and creek banks. Illustration by Larry Smail.

I believe a large number of whitetails are lost by bow and gun hunters each year. Certainly a large percentage of these are only superficially wounded, causing recovery to be impossible. If a deer doesn't die from the wounds it received, it can't be found. However, I feel there is a portion of the deer harvest that could have been recovered, but wasn't.

A hunter will often feel remorse for the deer he has killed. I have suffered this feeling on occasion, as have most other hunters, as it is human nature. Some of us think about the possible pain the deer endured before death, and some do not hunt because of this.

Many hunters wonder if a deer does feel pain. Unfortunately, it has been determined that they do. However, not having the more complex brain that we do, they tolerate a considerably greater amount of pain. A human shot through the stomach would probably moan and groan until death or loss of consciousness. We are able to reason and notice the fear that comes over us. I do not believe the whitetail is capable of comprehending a fear of death, as we would be. An animal has a strong will to survive, and this probably enables it to handle pain.

I feel many whitetails go into shock long before death, depending of course on the nature and severity of the wound. A hunter might feel better knowing the animal did not suffer until the time of death.

Hunters have come upon wounded deer still alive, and have not been able to properly dispose of the animal. Guilty feelings have taken over and they try to help the animal. I have experienced this feeling and it isn't pleasant. One veterinarian I spoke with has had deer hunters bring in wounded deer for treatment, usually deer that are six moths old, fawns of that year. I do not blame a hunter for taking a young deer if it is legal, and in many areas this is the case, particularly during the earlier archery seasons. But when a hunter chooses to shoot at a particular deer, he has made a commitment. Once a deer is wounded and you are able to approach it while it is still alive, you must properly dispose of the animal. It is your responsibility, as well as the humane thing to do.

The deer, as with any downed animal, should be approached from behind. It can be dangerous to walk up to a deer you thought was dead, only to have it spring to its feet when you touch it. I heard of a Kentucky deer hunter who had knocked down a buck on one clean rifle shot. He walked over to the buck and hollered for his friend who was hunting nearby. A few minutes later the friend arrived and offered to take pictures. As the hunter who shot the deer put a hand on each antler, the buck came to life and chucked the hunter aside, sprang to its feet and was gone. Fortunately neither hunter was hurt, but they never saw hide nor hair of the deer again.

It is best to poke the deer with a stick, your bow or whatever is handy. This may draw movement if there is still life left. Pay close attention to the deer's eyes, as shortly after death they begin to glaze, almost like a film is covering them. Be extra careful with larger bucks as an antler can do a number on you quickly.

Many trailing techniques discussed in this book will be helpful with mule deer, elk, moose, or other large game. Types of terrain may change your trailing style, but the information will help in many situations.

I feel that if you have read this book in its entirety, you have learned a great deal. I know that actual trailing in the field is the best experience you can get, but I believe this book will help you get there a little sooner.

Throughout this book I have told it like it is. As I mentioned in the introduction, I did not leave out the suffering. So many hunters and organizations have pushed aside the real facts of trailing. If we are going to hunt, there are deer that will undergo distress because of us. This part of it goes right along with the hunting.

I do feel the hunter who has been made aware of the cold, hard facts will be a better hunter. He will be more prone to take better shots, be more conscious of foolish choices and put an all-out effort into recovery.

At the beginning I said, "It is not always the blood trail that will lead you to the deer, for it is so often the effort you put forth." I believe nothing is closer to the truth. You have to be determined. If you feel strongly that you can find a deer, then you are almost there. Not giving up is what it's all about.

I am saddened that this book is now complete. Although it has taken a great deal of work and time to prepare and write, it has also been enjoyable to relate my experiences as I write. This archery season will begin in a few weeks and I expect to partake of new experiences. I am sure there is much more to learn.

GOOD TRAILING

Large or small—isn't it all worth it?
Photo by Dean Stallion.